GERMAN VEHICLES IN WORLD WAR II
Trucks of
the Wehrmacht
A Photo Chronicle

Reinhard Frank

Tanks, tractors, Opel Blitz, Steyr 1.5-ton, VW Kübel, light and medium uniform Pkw, of the "Grossdeutschland" Panzergrenadier Division — all waiting at the Tim River crossing in June of 1942 and providing a microcosm of the vehicles of an elite German division. "Normal" units had a far greater variety of vehicles!

GERMAN VEHICLES IN WORLD WAR II
Trucks of the Wehrmacht
A Photo Chronicle

Reinhard Frank

Schiffer Military History
Atglen, PA

Translated from the German by Dr. Edward Force.

This book was originally published under the title,
Lastkraftwagen der Wehrmacht,
by Podzun-Pallas Verlag.

Printed in the United States of America.
ISBN: 0-88740-686-6

We are interested in hearing from authors with book ideas on related topics.

Published by Schiffer Publishing Ltd.
77 Lower Valley Road
Atglen, PA 19310
Please write for a free catalog.
This book may be purchased from the publisher.
Please include $2.95 postage.
Try your bookstore first.

CONTENTS

On the unpaved roads of Russia, the supply troops had the hardest job to do. Here in the picture, even the German truck with the greatest off-road capability, the so-called Uniform Diesel, with six-wheel drive, got stuck, and had to be towed out, along with the Zündapp motorcycle, by a tracked vehicle. Note the interesting lettering on the fender; the big K for Panzer Group 1 (von Kleist), the tactical symbol for a howitzer battery (motorized platoon), and the number 6; on the door are the symbol of the 16th Panzer Division (yellow), and the symbol for ammunition truck 2. (BA)

Foreword

The supply troops of the German Army were aware of their responsible tasks at all times and always tried to fulfill them, even with insufficient means. Difficult demands, pushing their performance to its limits, were met with noteworthy organizational skill and improvisation.

Windisch, Generalmajor a.D. and General of the Supply Troops of the Field Army from July 1, 1943 to the war's end.

This book reports in depth on this neglected area of the German military of World War II. The units of the Wehrmacht are treated; the considerable supply organizations of the SS, NSKK, RAD, etc., could not be included in the framework of this book. The photo section and appendix deal in depth with the transport vehicles of the Wehrmacht.

Along with the usual open trucks, motor buses, combat vehicles, special bodies and the like will also be shown. Only a little about the "Maultier" halftrack is included. The usually well-known histories of the firms were deliberately kept brief, so as not to unduly limit the space for illustrations.

A particular need was the portrayal of at least a part of the countless types of captured vehicles, without which the supplying of the troops simply would not have been possible. The choice of the German manufacturers was made on the basis of 1936, for which reason Austrian and Czech trucks appear under "captured vehicles."

Identification of the vehicles was done through reference to all available specialized literature. As every aficionado knows, a precise identification of truck types is very difficult, often impossible — particularly when important identifying marks are missing or hidden.

Most of the photos came from former soldiers. Weaknesses in terms of sharpness, lighting and choice of subject must unfortunately be accepted if one does not want to get along without irreplaceable subject matter.

In the text, some information is reproduced directly from contemporary sources and "Feldgrau" in order to share the terminology of the times with the reader.

Special thanks go to my wife Gertrud, Messrs. Henry Hoppe and Peter Taghorn, as well as Bart Vanderveen for his kind assistance in identifying captured trucks.

Reinhard Frank
Gilching, Autumn 1992

Abbreviations

A-Typ = Allradgetrieben (all-wheel drive)
gp. = gepanzert (armored)
gl. = geländegängig (off-road capable)
gf. = Geländefähig (off-road capable)
HWA = Heereswaffenamt (Army Weapons Office)
Krad. = Kraftrad (motorcycle)
Kfz. = Kraftfahrzeug (motor vehicle)
Kom. = Kraftomnibus (motor bus)
Kw. = Kraftwagen (motor vehicle)
Lkw. = Lastkraftwagen (truck)
l. = leicht (light)
m. = mittel (medium)
(o) = handelsüblich (stock, production)
OKW = Oberkommando der Wehrmacht (military high command)
OHL = Oberste Heeresleitung = (supreme army command)
Pkw. = Personenkraftwagen (car, passenger vehicle)
Sd.Ah. = Sonderanhänger (special trailer)
Sd.Kfz. = Sonderkraftfahrzeug (special vehicle)
S-Typ = Standardtyp (rear drive)
s. = schwer (heavy)
Sanka = Sanitätskraftwagen (ambulance; also Sankra)
3-Tonner = Truck with 3-ton load
(6 x 4) = 4 wheels of 6 are driven (also double wheels)

(Note: most abbreviations were used both with and without a period (Lkw/Lkw.).

With such road signs, the drivers always knew where they were going. This one was seen in Szycheva in November 1941.

Photos and Documents provided by:

Mr. Nilges of the Federal Archives in Koblenz, Emil Burkhardt, Friedrich Birkmeyer, Horst Beiersdorf, Siegfried Bunke of the German Museum in Munich, Johann Demleitner, Siegfried Ehrt, Robert Emmert, Michael Foedrowitz, Heinz Friedrich, Heinrich Göttsche, Henry Hoppe, Ludwig Heymann, Sepp Herz, Helmut Heinrich, Georg Jagolski, Randolf Kugler, W. Leopold, Friedrich Masch, Ernst Obermaier, Peter Petrick, Pionierarchiv in Munich, Matthias Roth, Horst Scheibert, Franz Sindler, Johann Strauss, Peter Steger, Siegfried Stenger, Helmuth Spaether, Steve Schmidt, Peter Taghon, Hans Thudt, Bart Vanderveen, Heinz Wrobel, Albert Wörnle, Georg Wurm, and many others.

The Supply Troops of the Wehrmacht Historical Development

In World War I, the supplying of the troops at the front was done by the "ammunition columns and trains", all of which were horse-drawn. Transportation over longer distances was carried out by train or special motor vehicle units. The latter belonged to the transport troops and were directly subordinate to the supreme army leadership and not the "Commander of the Mun.Kol. and Trains." In all, some 40,000 standard trucks, made by a variety of firms, were produced, and some were rebuilt as, among others, artillery tractors and weapons carriers. The tremendous need for materials in the battles of World War I showed very clearly the importance of motorized supply transport. With growing distances, huge masses and fast speeds, the horse-drawn column became more and more outmoded.

A 50 HP Hansa-Lloyd truck, first built in 1917 to carry a load of 3 to 4 tons. For lack of rubber (there was no Buna synthetic rubber then), the front wheels are fitted with sprung railroad tires. This bone-shaking makeshift solution required additional springs and chain drive instead of a driveshaft.

This was naturally clear to the responsible parties in the Reichswehr, so that an extensive program of motorization was instituted in 1926.

According to the law of March 16, 1935 for the establishment of the Wehrmacht, the former driver training command of the Hannover Cavalry School was expanded that October to include a transport and a supply school, each with a supply driver training squadron and a supply driving company. On October 12, 1937 this part of the Cavalry School became the independent Army Supply School at the same site, with the driver training squadron and the driver training company. On November 15, 1938 this was renamed the Driving Troop School, and finally, on April 1, 1939, a second Driver Training Company was established. The unification of the three training units into one driver training unit was planned for the autumn of 1939, but the beginning of war prevented it from taking place.

The establishment of new units took place very slowly when measured by the considerable yearly growth rates of almost all other branches. The image of the transport troops, which then belonged to the so-called "back-line services", certainly played an important role, influenced by the spirit of the times. Compared to the preferentially treated classic service arms, it had a much more difficult time obtaining sufficient commissioned and non-commissioned officers.

On October 1, 1935, along with the training troop, Motor Vehicle Unit 7 (Munich) was established within the framework of the motorized combat troops; at first it included two companies and had an average strength of 442 soldiers as a corps troop of the VIIth Army Corps. The cadre of personnel for this first peacetime unit of the new supply troops came about 50% from the driving school of the Bavarian State Police (L.P.) in Munich and the Bavarian L.P. Motor Vehicle Department in Munich and Nürnberg, with a few from the Prussian L.P. The unit commander came from the Driver Training Command in Hannover; other personnel came from the Engineer Battalion Ingolstadt B (later No. 17). Such a mixture was not at all unusual at that time, but quite typical of numerous new units, including those of other service arms.

The organizational plan for the Army had as its first goal the establishment of one active motor vehicle unit for every three companies in each of the twelve (13 since 1937) defensive zones in the Reich at that time. This goal, in a peacetime army whose strength had risen by then to some 750,000 men, could not be attained by the time war broke out in 1939.

Out of Motor Vehicle Unit 7 there arose, through division and transfers from other troop units:

Motor Vehicle Units:

No. 1: Stablak	No. 9: Hersfeld
No. 3: Rathenow	No. 10: Hamburg
No. 6: Dortmund	No. 12: Bensheim-Speyersdorf
No. 7: Munich	No. 17: Enns
No. 8: Sprottau	No. 18: Bregenz

Transport Units:

No. 14: Bartenstein
No. 24: Hannover

All units (except No. 17 and 18 with two each) now had three companies, and the two horse-drawn units had three squadrons each.

The establishment of the still lacking Motor Vehicle Units 2, 4, 5, 11 and 13, with two companies each at first, was ordered for the autumn of 1939, but was prevented by the outbreak of the war.

From the weak peacetime cadres, transport units had to be organized for the numerous divisions and corps of the field army, for armies and army troops, fortress troops, border protection and patrol, as well as for the replacement army, when the war broke out. Of all types of troop units, the supply troops necessarily had the highest expansion quota. At most, there was one non-commissioned officer and two men of active personnel available for every unit to be organized hastily, as the active motor vehicle units, with their personnel and materials, had to be used primarily for the motor transport units of the army troops (three regiments and one other unit).

With a specified mobilization strength of 2,741,064 men for the field army, 191,088 (6.9%) belonged to the supply or administrative services, including the motor vehicle servicing units. In the replacement army there were 53,300 men out of 965,040 (5.5%).

With the growth of the wartime army and the extension of the theaters of war, the supply units also had to expand in both numbers and types. Combat areas with extreme climatic conditions, such as northern Finland or North Africa, caused additional extraordinary demands on which no one had reckoned in peacetime.

In December of 1943 the supply troops, with a total strength of the field army of 4,270,000 men, had some 350,000 men (including 20,000 officers), thus reaching its highest number of personnel.

On September 30, 1943 the divisions of the Wehrmacht included, among others, the following supply units:

181 staff of division supply leaders, 180 division supply companies
54 motor vehicle companies (120 t), 84 (90 t), 6 (60 t), 62 motor vehicle columns (26 of them large),
13 fuel columns
85 driving squadrons or large driving columns, 398 driving columns, 285 light driving columns, 13 mountain car columns, 2 pack animal columns
157 repair shop companies, 22 repair shop platoons
183 division food supply offices, 173 bakery companies, 10 bakery half-companies,173 butcher companies, 10 butcher half-companies
166 horse-drawn medical companies, 132 motorized, 2 horse-drawn medical half-com panies
302 Kranken-Kraftwagenzüge
176 veterinary companies, 6 veterinary platoons or echelons
177 field police troops (motorized)

The Tasks of the Back-Line Services

For the sake of authenticity, the following text was taken extensively from the supply guide-book of 1938 and the motor vehicle column guidebook of 1937.

Transport of Higher Leadership
To carry out the supplying of the field army, the higher command staffs have available:

the railroad
the shipping
the back-line services.

The back-line services are applied primarily in the operational area and serve to supply the fighting troops in all areas of supply. According to their various tasks, they are divided into:

Supply services   Veterinary services
Administrative services Order-keeping services
Medical services   Field postal services
Supply Services

Supply Services

Supply services (in the framework of the back-line services of a division) are not only supply columns, which might be taken from the designation: they carry not only ammunition, fuel, food, equipment, etc., in columns, but they also provide mobile workshops and repair service for damaged motor vehicles, weapons and equipment of all kinds, and at the same time provide a work force to load and unload columns and supply trains, set up distribution points, stores, parks, ect.

The troop leader of the "supply services" is the supply leader of the division, the corps, or the army. As a specialist in the quartermaster group, he recommends the utilization of the supply units led by him to the command offices. The carrying out of smooth supplying of the troops in the operations area depends essentially on frictionless cooperation between him and the other specialists in the division or other command staffs (commissariat officer, specialist for ammunition, infantry or artillery equipment, etc.). Constant phone communication between the division supply leader at the division staff and the masses of his supply units during movement, rest and quartering is absolutely necessary for the immediate use of the columns in establishing advanced fuel depots, ammunition distribution points, and beginning the activity of vehicle repair platoons.

The supply services can be divided into:

a) Supply columns
b) Motor vehicle columns for fuel supply
c) Repair shop companies
d) Field workshops (Army)
e) Supply companies and battalions
f) Motor parks (Army)

A bakery company (motorized) on the march near Göttingen on March 12, 1940 – truly with all kinds of vehicles: Austro-Fiat with bakery trailer (Sd.Anh. 106), Büssing-NAG, Ford semi-trailer, and finally an off-road three-axle truck.(BA)

Supply Columns:
They supply ammunition, food, weapons, clothing, equipment, war materials and army supplies of all kinds, and transport weapons and equipment in need of repair, captured and empty goods (fired ammunition, packing material, casings, cartridges), and in special cases also wounded and ill persons and animals.

Motor Vehicle (Kw.) Columns:
are divided into small columns with 30-ton load limit on ten medium or heavy trucks, and large columns with 60-ton load limit in 20 medium or heavy trucks.

Equipment of a Small Supply Column with 30-ton Load Limit:

a) with vehicles:

1 to 2 cars
1 to 2 motorcycles
2 groups of trucks, each with a total load limit of 15 tons, and a third group (Wirtschaftsgruppe) of 3-ton capability.

b) with personnel:

1 officer as leader
1 Oberfeldwebel, also deputy leader
3 non-commissioned officers as group leaders
1 to 2 car drivers
1 to 2 motorcycle drivers
1 leader and 1 aide for each truck, one of the aides as cook, another as emergency stretcher bearer.

Equipment of a Large Supply Column with 60-ton Load Limit:

a) with vehicles:

2 cars
2 motorcycles
4 groups of trucks, each with a total load limit of 15 tons, and a 5th group (Wirtschaftsgruppe), consisting of
2 fuel and equipment trucks, each of 3-ton load limit, and
1 medium truck to carry food and baggage.

b) with personnel:

1 officer as leader
1 Oberfeldwebel, also deputy leader
5 non-commissioned officers as group leaders,
1 medical non-commissioned officer
2 car drivers
2 motorcycle drivers
1 food supply man as train leader
1 driver and 1 aide for each truck, one of the aides as cook.

Horse-Drawn Columns
with total load limit of 30 tons on 40 two- or one-horse field wagons or typical native vehicles.

The motor vehicle columns (as long as they have no off-road vehicles) are limited to good, firm roads. Compared to horse-drawn columns, they have the following advantages: five times greater speed (25-30 kph), five to six times greater range (150 and more km per day), and a much smaller need for personnel.

The possibility of using horse-drawn vehicles across country, away from good, firm roads and paths, in rough country and unfavorable weather conditions — that put limits on the performance capability of motor vehicle columns — makes the retention of horse-drawn wagons for part of the supply column, as well as for the transportation of the combat troops (combat, food and other vehicles) absolutely necessary at first. If necessary, draft oxen are suitable for use if horses are lacking or because of the particular nature of the country.

Columns of pack animals are used to carry supplies in the mountains, where the use of horses and wagons is impossible. A pack animal carries 50-80 kg of load. The total load limit of a pack animal column, depending on the carrying ability of the animals and the terrain, can be up to five tons. In favorable terrain, at distances up to 15 km and altitudes up to 600-800 meters, on good cart tracks with grades of no more than 15%, small field wagons, mountain carts and sleds can also be used. In trackless mountain areas, columns of carriers instead of pack animals are foreseen.

Small and Large Vehicle Columns for Fuel
with a carrying capacity of 25 or 50 cbm, complete the need for motor vehicles by the staffs and troop units of the fighting troops as well as the back-line services in delivering gasoline, tires, oil, etc.
The vehicle repair platoons (division) provide short-term repair work for motor vehicles; the field repair shops (army) and armorer platoons (division) repair weapons and army equipment.
Motor vehicle repair and armorer platoons form the repair shop company.

Supply Companies (division) or Battalions (army), divided into ammunition, rations, gathering and technical platoons, provide the work force at unloading depots, motor parks and distribution points, so that drivers and aides of the columns and trains are generally not needed for loading purposes. The time of loading and unloading is used by the drivers for overhauling and testing of vehicle, motor, horses, equipment, etc.

Parks hold supplies of weapons and army equipment to replace equipment of the troops that is out of action because of loss, enemy action, damage, etc. If need be, branch parks can be advanced. The supplying of equipment from the army's unloading depots, parks and field repair shops to the troops (division equipment collecting points) is directed by the chief quartermaster (O.Qu.) at the staff of the A.O.K. In special cases, the troops receive replacement equipment at the aforementioned back-line facilities of the army.

Subordination of the Supply Columns (1939)

According to their use and affiliation with the command staffs, one can differentiate:

Army Supply Columns: They form a transport reserve of the Army High Command for army supplying. They are assigned by the Quartermaster General (Gen.Qu.) to armies, corps and divisions according to need, or in special cases placed under the direct command of the Quartermaster General (to replace railroads in case of damage, interruption, etc.).

Supply Columns of an Army serve that army to keep a portion of the supplies of ammunition, rations, etc., in motion, keep the army's supply dumps and parks filled regularly, and beyond that, to complete or support the supply services of the divisions subordinate to the army.

An army commissary store (AVL) in Bonn on November 6, 1939: The trucks of the affiliated Army and Luftwaffe units are being loaded.(BA)

Corps Supply Columns generally supply only their own corps' troops with ammunition, rations, etc.

The corps supply columns of a cavalry corps command, which are given distant marching destinations as a rule, carry a certain amount of ammunition and food (particularly oats) with them and are frequently used to assist the cavalry division's supply columns.

Division Supply Columns form a bridge between the back-line facilities of the army and the distribution points of the division.

Column Units: When the divisions advance, the division's supply columns are generally combined with parts of the other back-line services to form a Marching Unit, and sent to follow the motorized units of the combat troops under the command of an officer from the staff of the division supply leader.

Parts of the division's supply columns carrying artillery ammunition are combined into a combat unit and moved closer to the battlefield. In this situation they fill the ammunition needs of the batteries, etc., immediately on orders from the artillery commander of the division.

Structure of the Back-Line Services in the Division

Supply Services/Supply Troops

(Specified strengths, which varied greatly in individual divisions

1939-1941	1942-1945

Infantry Division

1939-1941	1942-1945
Staff Div. Supply Leader	Staff Cmdr, Div. Supply Troop
6 small vehicle col. 30 t each	1-3 vehicle comp. 90 t each
1 small fuel column, 30 t	
1 vehicle repair platoon	1 vehicle repair platoon
1-2 wagon columns, 30 t each	1-3 wagon squads, 60 t each
1 supply co. (t-mot), 3 platoons	1 supply co. (t-mot), 3 platns.
1 ammunition command at division supply leader	1 ammunition command at staff

Infantry Division (mot.)

1939-1941	1942-1945
10 small veh. col. 30 t each	4 vehicle co., 90 or 120 t each
1 supply co. (mot.), 2 platoons	1 supply co. (mot.), 2 platoons

Panzer Division

1939-1941	1942-1945
10 small veh. col., 30 t each	5-8 veh. co., 90 or 120 t each
1 supply co. (mot.), 2 platoons	1 supply co. (mot.), 2 platoons

Mountain Division

1939-1941	1942-1945
4-6 small veh. col., 30 t each	2 vehicle co., 90 or 120 t each
2-3 mtn. veh. co., 30 t each	4 mtn. veh. co., 30 t each
1 mtn supply co (t-mot), 3 pltns.	1 mtn. supply co (t-mot), 3 platoons

Jäger Division

1939-1941	1942-1945
3-4 small veh. col., 30 t each	1 vehicle company, 120 tons
2-3 vehicle columns, 30 t each	3 mtn. vehicle col., 30 t each
1 supply co. (t-mot), 3 platoons	1 supply co. (t-mot), 3 platns.

Average Strengths

	Officers	NCO	Men	Vehicles	Horses	Wagons
Vehicle Company	2	14-17	74-95	45-88	–	–
Wagon Squadron	2	19	190	1	203	82
Supply Co. (mot.)	2	14	105	14	–	–
Supply Co. (t-mot.)	2	22	151	8	10	5
Mtn. Supply Company	2	14	173	–	19	8

Administrative Services, divided into:
1 Commissariat (3 trucks, 1 car, 1 cycle)
1 Bakery company (24 trucks, 5 cars, 6 cycles)
1 Butcher platoon (6 trucks, 1 car, 2 cycles)

Medical Services, divided into:
1st Medical Company (horse-drawn) (1 truck, 1 car, 2 cycles, 17 wagons)
2nd Medical Company (mot.) (21 trucks, 4 cars, 6 cycles)
  1 Field hospital (11 trucks, 6 cars, 2 cycles)
  2 Ambulance platoons (each 15 ambulances, 2 cars, 8 cycles)

Veterinary Services, consisting of:
1 Veterinary company (9 trucks, 1 car, 3 cycles, 21 horse-drawn wagons)

Police Services, consisting of:
1 Field police troop (2 trucks, 2 cycles)

Field Postal Services, consisting of:
1 Field post office (2 trucks, 2 cars)

Chain of Command Within the Division

The supply units (back-line services) of a division were subordinate to the 2nd General Staff Officer (Ib), who was to manage this area according to the instructions of the 1st General Staff Officer Ia).

The supply services were subordinate to the Division Supply Leader (Dinafü), who received his instructions from the Ib.

The leader of the administrative services was the Division Commissariat Officer (IVa).

The medical services were subordinate to the Division Doctor (IVb), the veterinary services to the Division Veterinarian (IVc).

The police and postal services were directly subordinate to the Ib.

Transportation of the Combat Troops (Trains)

To carry out supplying on the advance, during combat or at rest, the infantry, artillery and other regiments were equipped with horse-drawn and motorized vehicles according to their organization, so that a part of their supplies of ammunition, food and materials of all kinds, equipment, baggage, etc., will be mobile and can be carried along, simultaneously guaranteeing two-way supplying between the front and the back-line facilities of the division (ammunition, food, fuel distribution points, equipment collecting places, etc.).

According to their tasks, the following can be differentiated:
        the combat train,
        the commissary train,
        the baggage train, and
        the light columns.

The Combat Train is composed of the combat vehicles (ammunition units), the field kitchen and the horses.

The Combat Vehicles (generally horse-drawn) take everything that the troops need to the battlefield: ammunition and war materials of all kinds, spare parts and tools for minor repairs, medical and veterinary equipment. On modern rubber-tired combat vehicles of the rifle companies, some of the marching packs of the men can also be carried.

On the march, the combat train is gathered in the battalion or other unit under the leadership of a non-commissioned officer (Oberfeldwebel or Futtermeister). When contact with the enemy is made, the combat wagons move at the end of their company, in prescribed marching order, under the leadership of the NCO for weapons and equipment. After the deployment of the rifle company, they follow their platoons (every platoon has one combat wagon).

All combat vehicles are drawn by two horses and driven from the seat or the saddle.

The Commissary Train

To carry out regular food supply service, all troop units have commissary vehicles which form the commissary train. The equipment of the individual troop units differs in number and type of vehicles, depending on whether or not the units are motorized.

a) Non-Motorized Troops

As a rule, every unit (company, etc.) has one commissary vehicle (field wagon or typical native wagon), every horse-drawn or mounted unit (machine-gun company, etc.) has two commissary or fodder wagons,every small unit (battalion, etc.) has one truck.

The horse-drawn wagons form the Commissary Train I (V.T.I), the trucks form the Commissary Train II (V.T. II).

When a unit marches out, the field kitchen carries the food supplies for that day. V.T.I carries the food for the next day and V.T. II carries the food for the day after that. In addition to these three daily portions of food, two portions of "iron rations" are carried (one by the field kitchen, one by the men).

Motorized Troops
The motorized units have only one truck for food transport – V.T. (mot.) – which can carry food for two days and, for this reason, is received only every other day at the food distribution point of the division. The V.T. (mot.) generally marches behind its troop unit if it is not underway to pick up food supplies and is recalled by special order in this situation. There is no division into Commissary Train I and II.

The Baggage Train

In the effort to free the combat troops of things that they do not absolutely need on the march or in battle, trucks have been assigned to all troop units according to plan. Some 75% of the entire baggage is carried on these trucks. The men have the remaining 25% to carry as their marching packs. They are urged to leave the greatest part of their marching packs (coat, blanket, etc.) on the combat wagon.

On the march, the baggage train is organized by regiment and division and follows the division at some distance.

The Light Columns

For constant resupplying of ammunition, war materials and equipment of all kinds, the regiments etc. have, in addition to the combat vehicles (combat wagons, limbers, ammunition units), light columns as well. They form the link between the troops (combat wagons, ammunition units) and the means of transport (supply columns) or facilities (ammunition distribution points) of the division. The light columns bring their troop units supplies of ammunition, close-combat equipment, hand grenades, explosives and fuses, flare and signaling ammunition, means of camouflage and equipment according to particular plans. According to their affiliation, they are divided into:

> light infantry columns
> light cavalry columns
> light artillery columns
> light engineer columns
> light intelligence columns

On the march, the light infantry columns generally march at the end of the main body in the order of their troop units; the motorized light engineer and other columns follow the main body at a greater distance in a "motorized echelon."

In place of the light artillery columns, the ammunition echelons of a division's artillery form the link between the batteries and the division's supply columns.

Renaming the Back-Line Services

In June of 1941 the "back-line services" were renamed "supply troops" in recognition of their accomplishments:

– Army Information Sheet HM 1941, No. 600:

Effective immediately, in place of the concept "back-line services", the term "supply troops" is to be used. The other designations, such as supply services, medical services, etc., remain unchanged.

OKH (Ch.H. Rüst und BdE), 6/4/1941

(New) Structure of the Troops of the Field Army, 1942

In the autumn of 1942, a new structuring of the service arms was made by the OKH. This status was made known in HM 878 of 10/14/1942.

The "supply services" were now named "supply troops." The following "complete" list was published:

The troops of the field army are divided into:

Combat Troops
Supply Troops
Security Troops

1. To the <u>Combat Troops</u> there belong:
a) the command offices
b) the infantry
c) the armored troops
d) the artillery
e) the engineers (including construction and roadbuilding troops)
f) the foglaying troops
g) the intelligence troops
h) the railroad troops
i) the technical troops
j) the propaganda troops
k) the railroad transport troops
l) the map and survey troops
m) the fortress cadre troops
n) the front reconnaissance troops
o) the secret field police (parts)

2. The <u>Supply Troops</u> are divided into:
a) the supply troops
b) the administrative troops
c) the medical troops
d) the veterinary troops
e) the ordnance troops
f) the motor park troops
g) the water supply troops
h) the police troops
i) the field postal system

2.1 To the <u>Supply Troops</u> there belong:
– Motor transport troops, high commander of the supply troops (army group supply leader), commander of the army supply troops, commander of the corps supply troops, commander of the division supply troops
– Motor transport units (regiments) and independent units for large-scale transport areas (GTR)
– Supply staffs z.b.V.
– Supply column units, motorized (6 col. each 60 tons) and horse-drawn (renamed Kraftfahr-, Kw-Transport or Fahrabetilungen in 1942).

– Supply battalions, motorized and horse-drawn (0-1 motorized and 2-4 horse-drawn companies each)
– Independent vehicle (supply), horse-drawn and pack-animal columns with 10-60-ton capacity
– Motor vehicle companies with 60, 90, 120 and more tons of carrying capacity
– Company columns (10 buses each, also units with 3 columns, plus front aid columns of the German Reichspost
– Vehicle squadrons (30-90 tons) (former vehicle columns, 1942-43), plus mountain vehicle columns, pack-animal columns, etc.
– Ammunition administration companies (to field troops, 1943)
– Fuel administration companies
– Fuel filling companies and commands
– Supply companies for fuel
– Weapon repair companies and platoons
– Engineer park battalions
2.2 To the Administrative Troops there belong:
  Food offices, bakery and butcher companies, Army commissary services, Army housing authorities, Army construction services, clothing offices and stores, clothing instructional staffs, clothing repair trains.
2.3 To the Ordnance Troops there belong:
  Ordnance staffs, captured weapon staffs, ordnance battalions, Army equipment parks
2.4 To the Motor Park Troops there belong:
  Repair shop companies, motor parks, spare-parts stores, towing platoons
2.5 To the Water Supply Troops there belong:
  Battalion staffs for water supply, light and heavy water supply companies, distillation companies, filter companies, small and large water columns
2.6 To the Police Troops there belong:
  Guard battalions, bicycle guard battalions, field police
2.7 To the Field Postal Service there belong:
  Army field postmasters, field post direction points, field post offices
3. The units of the Security Troops cannot be dealt with within the framework of this book.

The Supply Troops 1944/45

As of the autumn of 1944, the supply troops of the front divisions were gradually gathered into Division Supply Regiments (with staff and staff company), whereby the supply troops formed a supply-troop unit, the administrative troops an administrative-troop unit. The medical unit, motor park troops, sometimes a veterinary company, and the field post office likewise belonged. Panzer and motorized divisions were assigned not only two or three vehicle repair companies but also a spare-parts echelon (75 t). The extent and composition of these regiments depended on the types of the various division units and thus showed many variations; precise data are lacking.

Toward the end of the war, there usually remained only one motor vehicle company (120 tons), two wagon squadrons (30 tons), one supply column and one administrative company (with commissary, bakery and butcher components) in the infantry divisions, which had grown smaller for lack of men and material. The last divisions of the 35th Wave, established in March 1945, each had two weak infantry regiments and could be given only one vehicle column (30 tons), one wagon squadron (30 tons) and one administrative company.

According to an Army memorandum of the OKW of 10/27/1944, the "Transport Corps Speer" was also assigned to the Wehrmacht. It included:

1. NSKK Transport Group Todt (consisting of the former NSKK Transport Brigade Speer and NSKK Transport Brigade Todt),
2. Legion Speer,
3. Transport Fleet Speer.

The members of the Transport Corps Speer were divided into:
a) uniformed "corps members" and
b) civilian "follower members."

Large Transport Area (GTR)

The largest independent transport unit of the field army was the "Grosstransportraum" (GTR), which was directly subordinate to the General of the Supply Troops.

The basis of the GTR was formed by the Motor Vehicle Transport Regiments 602, 605 and 616, the last two originally designated "Commercial Vehicle Transport Regiments."

The Kw.Tr.Rgt. 602 was formed of personnel and materials taken from all peacetime motor vehicle units and was the active regiment. It was divided into staff, staff company, field police platoon, three units of five companies each, a repair platoon and an information platoon, a total of sixteen companies. The regiment's transport vehicles were four-ton trucks with four-ton trailers. Its total strength, with a tonnage of 4500 tons, was 3000 men and 2200 vehicles, including motorcycles.

Regiments 605 and 616 had the same structure as the active Regiment 602, but except for a small cadre of active leaders and deputy leaders, were formed completely of men from industry, hence the name "Commercial Vehicle Transport Regiments." It had vehicles of the most varied types and sizes, not to mention ages and body types. They had only one thing in common: They were built exclusively for civilian use and certainly only for use on good roads.

For the most part, they were six- to ten-ton trucks with trailers, forming road trains with loads up to 20 tons. The tonnage of Regiment 605 was 6000 tons, that of Regiment 616 was 9000 tons.

The fuel consumption for 100 km of transit on roads was 50 cbm for the regiment, its marching speed in daylight and in good weather was 30 kph, at night 10 to 15 kph. The regiment had a marching depth of 40 km when opened up, and up to 120 km on the march. A day's marching including loading and unloading of goods, stops and rests, averaged 300 km, but at times individual performances achieved up to twice as much.

Special mention is deserved by the drivers of the GTR. Often called in with their own road trains, the long-distance drivers formed an elite of capable men. When the formation of new Panzer divisions was ordered in 1943-44, more than 10,000 officers, non-commissioned officers and men, a third of their total personnel, had to be provided by the GTR alone. They also proved themselves in the combat troops, especially as tank drivers. In the GTR there were over 1000 different makes and models of motor vehicles, which made maintenance tremendously difficult. Only in 1943 could some simplification of makes – but not models – be achieved, which necessitated exchanges among almost all theaters of war.

The GTR reached its highest tonnage, almost 80,000 tons, at the beginning of 1943, and remained at about 70,000 tons until 1944, with a work force of 35,000 men. It functioned in all theaters of war, with emphasis on the east. As a result of losses beginning in 1944, its tonnage that year sank to 60,000 tons, and amounted to about 45,000 tons by the end of the war.

After Germany surrendered, parts of the GTR remained in operation. Several thousand tons were still moving in Italy, other parts in Germany, to supply prisoner-of-war camps and the civilian population. Lowered to some 700 tons at the end of the war, it was raised to about 4000 tons by the British occupation forces and ran between the North Sea and the Alps until the summer of 1946.

Other than the vehicle transport units, various special formations, listed here briefly, belonged to the GTR:

– NSKK Regiment 5, with eight companies, subordinated only when in action, otherwise remaining under the NSKK.

– Two NSKK repair shops, superbly equipped, with highly trained personnel, who provided valuable service maintaining the GTR's motor vehicles.

– Columns of 10 buses each, capable of carrying 20 to 20 persons, intended for personnel or wounded transport. Each bus could carry two to three tons when used for shipping freight.

– Refrigerator columns, originally intended to transport meat.

When these were eliminated by the Army's customary fresh meat   supplies, they were likewise called on for supply transport.   But because of their heavy special bodies, they required paved   roads.

– Tanker columns (Kewa), 30 or 60 tons, individual capacity 2000 to 6000 liters of fuel.

– German Reichspost front assistance columns of ten buses each.

– Several commercial transport regiments of varying strength, but only available for military use toward the end of the war, and working for the civil authorities previously.

According to need, the following could also be provided:
– Supply staffs z.b.V.
– Construction battalions
– R.A.D. units
– O.T. columns

According to Generalmajor Windisch, whom we thank for this information, there were still certain units in action, regardless of losses and decreased tonnage:

– 12 vehicle transport staffs (not counting NSKK Regiment 5)
– 23 vehicle transport units of four 500-ton companies each (with two companies having no vehicles)
– 15 vehicle transport units of four 250-ton companies each (with seven companies having no vehicles)
– 19 motor vehicle units of six 180-ton companies each
– 4 motor vehicle companies "a" of 90 tons each
– 43 motor vehicle companies "b" of 120 tons each
– 10 motor vehicle companies "c" of 180 tons each
– 27 columns of 10 buses each
– 1 large tanker column of 60 tons
– 8 small tanker columns of 30 tons each
– 7 refrigerator columns of 60 tons each

The Trucks of the Wehrmacht

Overview

The greatest difficulty since motorizing of the German Army began was the great variety of makes and models. This resulted from the comparatively meager production capacities of the motor vehicle factories at that time, particularly in the 1920s.

The Reichswehr, on the basis of its experience in World War I, naturally wanted to get away from its strictly stock trucks, and in 1926, within the framework of the first motorizing program, it issued contracts for the building of off-road-capable three-axle (6 x 4) trucks.

In an effort not to overburden the individual firms, the contracts for the 1.5-ton trucks were divided among three firms:

Daimler-Benz (2000 G 3a), Büssing-NAG (2300 G 31), and Magirus (1150 M 206). These vehicles, to be sure, were completely alike externally, but it was completely impossible to interchange components among them.

There were even four firms that shared the building of the 3-ton off-road truck: Büssing-NAG (300 Type 3 GL 6), Krupp (about 2000 L 3 H 63), Daimler-Benz (7500 LG 3000 – large numbers of which were exported), and Henschel (25,800 Type 33D1 and G1, including those built under license by Magirus).

From the beginning, there were many possibilities for necessary standardization.

As of 1937, attempts were made to meet the requests of the troops by creating the light uniform truck, the "Uniform Diesel." Under the direction of the Army Weapons Office, this vehicle was built by several firms, with more than 10,000 trucks made completely identical. The Uniform Diesel, with its 6 x 6 drive and single tire type, had outstanding off-road capability, but (like the three uniform passenger vehicles), was too heavy and too expensive to build.

The construction of a medium and a heavy uniform truck was not pursued at first. For off-road use, the troops still had to make do with stock 4 x 2 and 4 x 4 trucks (the so-called completion vehicles).

Shortly before the war began, the well-known Schell Plan of the "Empowered General for Motor Vehicles" Oberst Adolf von Schell was put into effect. The plan called for a reduction from over 100 different truck types to fourteen basic types. Because of the difficult situation in the war, the Schell program was only carried out in part. It is remarkable that, despite the dictatorship of the time, the comparatively small but very stubborn German firms were not "standardized", as was done, for instance, with manufacturers in the USA and Canada. In these countries, a radical standardization resulted in tremendous mass production of high-quality motor vehicles: 500,000 of the GMC Type 353 alone were built, more than 200,000 of the Canadian Ford F60, etc.

According to "Deutsche Automobilindustrie", the German manufacturers built a total of 429,000 trucks for military use. There were also considerable numbers of vehicles captured or produced in occupied countries. Unfortunately, there are no reliable statistics available.

Production figures are always a strictly kept secret of all warring nations. On the basis of the following statistics, an overview of the capacities of German truck production before World War II can be provided. The figures are based on the year 1937, as later figures are not available.

Total: 321,000 civilian delivery and freight trucks
including: 83.3% with gasoline motors
12.3% with Diesel motors
0.3% with wood-gas generators

The chief manufacturers of trucks were:

Manufacturer	Percentage	Manufacturer	Percentage
Büssing-NAG	5.3%	MAN	2.0%
Daimler-Benz	9.5%	Opel	36.5%
Hansa-Lloyd-Goliath	12.4%	Pha"nomen	1.7%
Henschel	1.1%	Tempo	2.0%
Krupp	2.9%	Ford	16.8%
Magirus	3.5%	Others	6.3%

103,420 trucks had load capacities of 2.0 to 7.5 tons and thus were classified as completion vehicles for the Wehrmacht.

A German truck column returning from Romania in the spring of 1944. Recognizable is a Henschel Type 33 with Special Trailer 202, loaded with exhausted infantrymen instead of an 88 mm AA gun. (BA)

GERMAN TRUCKS

Carl F.W. Borgward GmbH, Bremen

The Borgward firm came into being in 1938 after a series of crises that resulted in owner-ship and name changes.

Originating from the NAMAG (1096-1914), the firm was called "Hansa-Lloyd-Werke AG" until 1931, "Hansa-Lloyd and Goliath-Werke, Borgward und Tecklenborg oHG" from 1931 to 1936, "Hansa-Lloyd-Goliath-Werke AG" from 1936 to 1938, and finally "Carl F.W. Borgward Automobil- und Motorenwerke GmbH" from 1938 to 1949.

Trucks with one- to five-ton load limits were built. The most important models for the Wehrmacht were the Type Europa V (Uniform Diesel), 2400 of which were built up to 1940, and the various three-ton types, 30,000 of which were built until the factory was destroyed in 1944.

BORGWARD-LKW mit den Truppen an den Kultstätten der Antike

The postal and railway trucks were constantly being requisitioned for transport duty by the Wehrmacht. This picture shows a Hansa-Lloyd Merkur of the German Railways, led by an Adler Type 3 Gd medium personnel vehicle of the Luftwaffe.

A two-ton Borgward with single rear wheels after being hit (WH-194 475).

A requisitioned civilian Borgward with 4- to 5-ton load being sent to the front.

The "Lkw 3 t Borgward Type 3 t Benzin G.W.", as portrayed in D 669/35 of 9/3/1941. The vehicle was portrayed as a medium truck, open (o), and had a 6-cylinder, 3.4-liter motor that produced 73 HP. This type generally had an open uniform cab.

This 3-ton Borgward of Engineer Battalion 7 came under Polish defensive fire on the Raba in 1939. The letter K by the tactical symbol means "engineer motor vehicle column." Note the Hansa-Lloyd monogram in the Borgward emblem! (BA)

A "Borgward Type 3 t Diesel G.W." of SS Armored Engineer Battalion 9 "Hohenstaufen" went off the road near Ypres in 1943. Note the 3-axle trailer that was possibly adapted from a uniform Diesel.

A "Borgward Type 3 t Benzin G.W." of an engineer unit near Minsk in the spring of 1942.

The 3-ton Borgward with box body and rigid cab was relatively rare. This is a vehicle of Panzer Observation Battery 322 (Later Pz.B.B. 90), which was subordinate to the 10th Panzer Division, equipped as Evaluation Vehicle Kfz. 62 with Special Trailer 23 (battery-charging device).

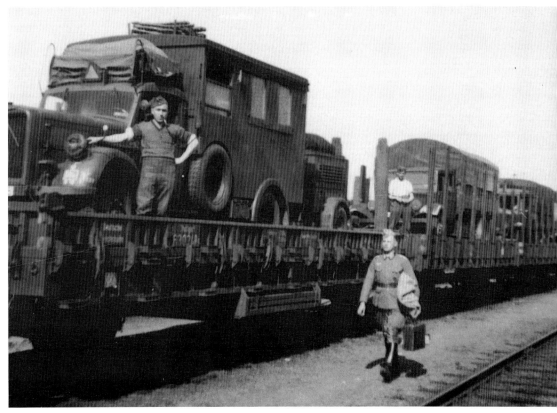

The further development of the Type G.W. was the "Lkw 3 t Borgward Type B 3000", which existed in A and S versions, and with 75 HP Diesel and 78 HP gasoline motors as of 1942. This picture shows a Borgward B 3000 S/D in southern Russia in the autumn of 1943. (BA)

A light 3-ton towing tractor (Special Vehicle 11) tows a Borgward Type B 3000 of the Waffen-SS through a ford in southern Russia.

A radio truck on the Borgward Type B 3000 chassis in North Africa.

Return of the 101st Infantry Division from the Nikopol area in 1943: Borgward Type B 3000 with box body, as an ambulance.

Büssing-NAG AG, Braunschweig

The firm of Heinrich Büssing is Germany's oldest truck manufacturer. Founded in 1903 as "Heinrich Büssing, Spezialfabrik for Motorlastwagen, Motoromnibusse und Motoren", it operated from 1920 to 1931 as "Heinrich Büssing Automobilwerke AG", from 1931 to 1943 as "Büssing-NAG, Vereinigte Nutzkraftwagenwerke AG", and from 1943 to 1950 as "Büssing-NAG Nutzkraftwagen GmbH."

The main factory was in Braunschweig; branches were in Berlin-Oberschöneweide, Elbing and Leipzig.

Büssing-NAG produced a variety of trucks with loads from 1.5 to 9.5 tons, mainly powered by Diesel engines of the firm's own manufacture.

The most important types for the troops were the G 31 (2300 made from 1931 on), the Uniform Diesel (3200, made until 1940), and in particular the Types 500/4500, of which almost 15,000 were made in S- or A- versions.

Advertisement for the Büssing-NAG Type 500 A (January 1942).

The 4.5-ton Büssing-NAG used the firm's own Type LD Diesel engine (6 cylinders, 7.4 liters, 105 HP). It was designated Type 500 A with all-wheel (4 x 4) drive, or Type 500 S for the standard (2 x 2) version. The front vehicle in the upper photo is a Type 500 A, recognizable by the tow hook mounted at the side and the short running board with the large gap to the door. The commissary truck shown below is the Type 500 S (towing hook on the bumper, smaller gap by the door). The vehicles belonged to S.R. 74 of the 19th P.D. and were photographed near Juknov in 1942.

A Navy road train with two trailers pulled by a Büssing-NAG Type 500 S with open cab (WM-105 225).

In March of 1941, Motor Vehicle Transport Regiment 602 moved the entire 1st Mountain Division from Besancon to the Yugoslavian border. The picture shows a Büssing-NAG Type 500 S with open cab transporting beasts of burden.

A Büssing-NAG Type 500 S with an additional opening in the rear body, as was seen, for example, in commissary trucks.

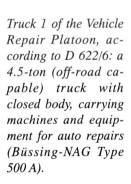

Truck 1 of the Vehicle Repair Platoon, according to D 622/6: a 4.5-ton (off-road capable) truck with closed body, carrying machines and equipment for auto repairs (Büssing-NAG Type 500 A).

Strakonice on 5/6/1945: A Büssing-NAG 4.5-ton truck with wood-gas drive, in Czech hands.

The Büssing-NAG Type 4500 was first available in 1942. It had a refined radiator grille and simplified cooling louvers. Later the bumper was eliminated and the front fenders became considerably thinner. This is the Type 4500 A of a V2 rocket battery, where it was listed as "Fahrzeug-Pos.-Nr. 508 Lkw 4.5 t geschl. als Sammler-Lkw (heizbar)", a battery truck with: 1 = heater, 2 = ventilator flap, 3 + tool chest. (Photo: German Museum, Munich)

A Büssing-NAG Type 4500 S with wooden cab, shortly after the end of the war.

Life went on. Many a shipper went into business in 1945 with a mustered-out military truck, such as these traditional Bavarians with a well-kept Büssing-NAG 4500.

Advertisement for the branch firm, gained in 1938, of A. Fross-Büssing in a Luftwaffe publication of 1943.

Some 300 of the Büssing-NAG Type III GL 6 (6 x 4) were built from 1931 to 1938. The vehicle had a 90 HP gasoline motor and a load limit of 2.5 tons. The picture shows a weather truck (Kfz. 72) or print shop truck (Kfz. 72).

A very rare vehicle in the Wehrmacht was the Büssing-NAG Type KD (6 x 4), 415 of which were built for export to Turkey from 1936 to 1938. The vehicle had a Büssing-NAG LD6 Diesel motor that produced 100 HP. The grille guard and the pierced bumper were typical of it. This vehicle belonged to the 1st Mountain Division.

Büssing-NAG Type KD of an unknown supply unit in Flanders in 1940.

A Büssing-NAG Type KD with light pontoon carrier (Pf. 15) of Engineer Battalion 3 near Kuyan on the Polish border in the autumn of 1939.

The motorized units preferred to advance along paved roads – the slow horse-drawn troops (here with the Hf 2 heavy field wagon) were forced into the ditches. The picture shows a 1.5-ton Büssing-NAG Type G 31 (6 x 4) as a telephone truck (Kfz. 77) in Poland in 1939. (BA)

Büssing-NAG Type G 31 as a limber truck (Kfz. 69) of the 14th Company of I.R. 79.

The Büssing-NAG Type G 31 was built from 1931 to 1936 and also used by the "Legion Condor" in Spain. Here is an orientation truck (Kfz. 61) with a one-axle navigation radio trailer (Sd.Anh. 422).

Büssing-NAG "Burglöwe" as a personnel vehicle of the 6th SS Mountain Division "Nord" in northern Finland.

A rebuilt Büssing-NAG "Burglöwe" moving van as an operating-room vehicle of the 45th I.D.

Choral near Kiev on 9/16/1941: Motorcycle riflemen of the 9th P.D. pass a Büssing-NAG 8-ton truck (4 x 2). This truck still has ventilating flaps instead of the louvers introduced in 1938.

A defensive position in Hungary, 1944: at left a 15 cm heavy Field Howitzer 18, in the foreground a civilian Büssing-NAG of an unidentified type. (BA)

A member of the Organization Todt works on a steel beam near the Minsk-Mogilev road. In the background, a Büssing-NAG 8.5-ton truck, Type 801 or 802, thunders by (6-cylinder Diesel engine, 110 or 145 HP, 12 liters, first built in 1933).(BA)

Daimler-Benz AG, Stuttgart-Untertürkheim

In 1926 the "Daimler-Motoren-Gesellschaft" in Untertürkheim and the "Benz u. Cie." in Mannheim merged to form the "Daimler-Benz AG", with its headquarters in Untertürkheim. The entire car and truck program continued under the name of "Mercedes-Benz."

The firm built technically advanced utility vehicles from 1.5 to 10 tons at Untertürkheim, Mannheim, Gaggenau and Berlin-Marienfelde.

Built especially for the troops were: the Type G 3 a (about 2000), the LG 3000 (7500), the "Uniform Diesel" (500), , the 4.5-ton truck in A- and S- versions (about 9000, including 1500 "Maultier" versions), and the Opel "Blitz" (about 3500), built under license.

Factory picture of the 4.5-ton Mercedes-Benz Type L 4500 A (4 x 4) truck, which was built from 1941 to the end of the war. The vehicle had a 6-cylinder, 7.20liter Diesel motor producing 122 HP.

The German troops withdrawing from Brussels (Sept. 2-3, 1944) were secretly photographed by a Belgian. The truck, full of soldiers, is towing a "Large Field Kitchen Hf. 13", which was intended to be horse-drawn. The light-colored camouflage paint and the aircraft observer (Lucki-Lucki) on the front fender are easy to see. The truck is a Mercedes-Benz Type L 4500, surely the S version, as one can tell by the recessed wheel hub at the front.

Toward the end of the war, the 4.5-ton Mercedes truck had also been slimmed down a lot: no bumper, primitive fenders, smaller headlights and a pressed-wood cab were its most noticeable identifying marks. This Type L 4500 S was heading for the Strakonice weapons factory on May 5, 1945, with a Czech crew.

Whoever had the good fortune not to be a prisoner of war after the war ended could found a flourishing business with a mustered-out Wehrmacht truck. This is a Mercedes-Benz Type L 4500 S with modernized cab and license number A/B 47-6553 for the American Zone of Bavaria, City of Munich.

A number of Mercedes-Benz Type L 4500 A trucks were fitted with a grille guard 8 mm thick and an armored cab. This picture shows a burned-out example in Belgium in 1944, carrying a 3.7 cm AA gun and towing an 8.8 cm AA gun.

The Mercedes-Benz Type LG 3000 (6 x 4) medium off-road truck (o) carried a load of 2.8 tons and had a Daimler-Benz Type OM 67 Diesel motor with 6 cylinders, 7.4 liters and 95 HP. This close-up of a vehicle of the 5th Co., Railway Engineer Regiment 3, was taken near Rostov and clearly shows the winch ahead of the rear wheels.

Rear view of a Mercedes-Benz Type LG 3000 towing a light Field Howitzer 15. To protect the wooden-spoke wheels of older guns ("hot."), they had to be moved on so-called rollbucks when towed by motor vehicles.

Mercedes-Benz Type LG 300 with double cab and lengthened bed to transport the launching racks of the heavy Wurfgerät 40. Note the removed strut ahead of the driver and the off-road chain "Special skidding protection for multi-axle motor vehicles") in a rack on the side of the rear body.

Thanks to a navigational error, these Luftwaffe soldiers landed their Mercedes-Benz Type LG 3000 in the midst of the fabled Westerwald. The winch on the side, the jack on the running board, the rope coil with its protective cover in front of the grille and one rope guide on the bumper are easy to see.

Two views of an "aviation fuel tank truck (Kfz. 384) with chassis of the medium off-road truck (o)", a Mercedes-Benz Type LG 3000 of J.G. 2, in northern France in 1942. Note the location of the exhaust pipe under the front bumper, customary for tank trucks, the slit cover of the main headlight, and the tires with the fairly uncommon "Wehrmacht tread." The tank had a capacity of 3500 liters of fuel.

The light off-road (o) Mercedes-Benz Type G 3 a (6 x 4) was built from 1929 to 1935 and had a 6-cylinder, 3.7-liter gasoline motor producing 68 HP. This picture shows a personnel truck (Kfz. 70) of the Engineer Completion Company of Ingolstadt during maneuvers on the Ammer in Upper Bavaria in 1936, still bearing a Reichswehr number.

The field kitchen, at least in the opinion of the troops, was far and away the most important military equipment. In order to be able to keep up with the motorized units, the kitchen equipment was completely mounted on off-road capable trucks, This is a Mercedes-Benz Type G 3 a (RW-33570) with a "large field cookstove (Fkh. 13)", that could provide 225 meals, mounted on it. The cover was lowered in the vicinity of the stove, to avoid the sparks from the mouth of the smokestack.

With its projecting springs and angular radiator, the Mercedes-Benz Type G 3 a looked somewhat old-fashioned. Its workmanship, though, was as highly praised as its off-road capability, and several vehicles remained in use till the war's end. This is a survey truck (Kfz. 64) of the 5th Co., Railway Engineer Regiment 3, with a flat tire on its way to the Caucasus in August 1942.

The same truck in Bukagitna (Jan. 4-12, 1942) without any winter camouflage. Note the covers with vertical slits on the small lights.

A Mercedes-Benz Type G 3 a from the formative years of the Wehrmacht, with box body and signal horn. This truck belonged to the 2nd Co., Intelligence Unit 7, and is marked "Kl.Fu.Kw. 3 (Kfz. 61)" and "Eigengewicht 3650 kg, Nutzlast 1250 kg." According to D 600, it is a "Radio truck (Kfz. 61)."

These red-painted Mercedes-Benz Type L 1000 express mail trucks (1926-34) of the Reichspost were used by Motor Ambulance Platoon 54 of the 1st Mountain Division as badly sprung ambulances (Kfz. 31), and are seen at the Dukla Pass in the autumn of 1939.

The Mercedes-Benz Type L 1500 S was built since 1937 with both 47 HP gasoline and 45 HP Diesel motors. The 1.5-ton truck was too small and uneconomical for military use. The picture shows a flatbed truck of SS Mountain Engineer Battalion 6 (Division "Nord") at the Pya Lake in northern Finland in the autumn of 1943.

A Mercedes-Benz Type L 1500 S, followed by an Opel Blitz commissary truck and the operations vehicle of an unknown Luftwaffe field hospital with the emblem of a chamois (similar to I./JG 51).

The all-wheel-drive 1.5-ton vehicle was listed in the appropriate specifications as both s.gl.Pkw and l.gl.Lkw. This Mercedes-Benz Type L 1500 A personnel car (Kfz. 70) was captured by the American 79th Fighter Group (P.40) in Tunisia in 1943.

At the railroad station in Holzkirchen, Upper Bavaria, just after the war ended: The Mercedes-Benz Type Lo 2000 or Lo 2500 (Lo = semi-low frame) has an unusual B/Y license number of transitional times. The worn-out 3.5-ton Citroen with wood-gas drive still shows a Wehrmacht number and the socket of the camouflage headlight. With these two trucks a clever entrepreneur gathered abandoned Wehrmacht vehicles, motors, scrap and the like.

Some 16,000 of the 3-ton Mercedes-Benz Type L 3000 S (4 x 2) truck were built from 1938 to 1944. The vehicle had an OM 65/4 Diesel engine (OM = oil motor): 4 cylinders, 4.8 liters, 75 HP. This vehicle, of a Luftwaffe field hospital, got stuck on the plains of southern Russia in 1942.

Factory photo of an all-wheel-drive Mercedes-Benz Type L 3000 A (4 x 4). The vehicle had the same motor as the S version, but the cab shown here did not go into production. An important identifying mark of front-wheel drive is, along with the front reduction gears, the massive stub of the front-wheel driveshaft, which is easy to see in this picture.

A Mercedes-Benz Type L 3000 carrying Romanian soldiers in the spring of 1944. By the attachment of the pick and shovel, this may well be the A version. Note the typical mount of the camouflage headlight and the Czech MG 26 gun. (BA)

Late June, 1941, just before the attack on Riga: Soldiers of Bicycle Battalion 402 get their food from the commissary truck, a Mercedes-Benz Type L 3000 S.

Mercedes-Benz Type O 2600 medium bus as "mammoth radio car" of the 3rd Co., Geb. N.A. 54, near Lemberg in 1941. The vehicle carried three radio troops with a 100-watt and a 5-watt transmitter, plus four "b" receivers. The "Klotz System" antenna was improvised. The bus, with body by the "Karosseriewerk Mannheim" had been captured in Yugoslavia with an odometer reading of 150 kilometers.

The requisitioned buses were generally used as spacious command cars. On Russian "roads" these vehicles, accustomed to paved streets, were naturally very overstrained. The picture shows a 42-passenger line bus, built about 1936, on Mercedes-Benz Type Lo 3750 chassis (100 HP Diesel engine), which had to be towed out by the Organization Todt in the Ukraine in 1942.

Mercedes-Benz Type L 3750 (WH-142 893) of an unknown unit (probably construction engineers) with building materials and cement mixers on the way to the West Wall. Road trains with two trailers, as seen here, reached a considerable length and caused a definite danger for the rest of the traffic. despite the warning triangle sign atop the cab. The L 3750 had a 6-cylinder, 7.2-liter, 100 HP Diesel engine and is easily recognizable by the Trilex front wheels.

At the beginning of the French campaign, the truck transport regiments were supplemented by Reichsbahn vehicles with an overall tonnage of more than 10,000 tons. Here such a road train of the Deutsche Reichsbahn, a Mercedes-Benz Type L 6500 with an open (o) multi-axle trailer, total tonnage up to 11 tons, is seen in a dangerous spot near Peronne. Unfortunately, this photo, from the 1st Mountain Division, includes no word as to how this bridge collapsed and the complete rear axle was torn out, or what role the French Panhard 178 played.

The Uniform Diesel
(various manufacturers)

The development of a "uniform chassis for light trucks", just like that of the light, medium and heavy uniform cars, answered the Wehrmacht leadership's urgent requests for a unification of the motor vehicle supply. Leading the way in technical development was the Army Weapons Office (HWa). The Type HWa 526 D (80 HP) Diesel engine was developed by MAN in collaboration with Henschel and Humboldt-Deutz. The chassis was planned chiefly by Henschel.

The "Uniform Diesel", as the vehicle was generally called, was built from 1937 to 1940 by MAN (ca. 1800), Henschel (ca. 1500). Magirus (ca. 2500), Büssing-NAG (ca. 3200), Faun (ca. 700), Daimler-Benz (ca. 550), and probably Vomag. The vehicle was technically advanced, robust and reliable. Because of its complex running-gear design (six-wheel drive and individual suspension of all wheels), the Uniform Diesel had remarkable off-road capability, and was thus very popular among the troops. One disadvantage was the low load limit of 2375 kg, compared to a net weight (ready to go, with a driver) of 4925 kg. Production was halted in 1940, as less expensive two-axle trucks with comparable performance figures existed by then.

A Uniform Diesel with tire chains on all six wheels, seen in a 1940 RuuD advertisement. The spare wheel is missing, thus the exhaust system is easy to see. The typical indentation in the right door was necessary to allow full opening of the door. Most vehicles had side panels of sheet steel rather than wood as here.

Advancing east of Smolensk in the summer of 1941: Uniform Diesels (obviously loaded with engineers' materials), with unusual German cross on the sides, pass the sight of a breakthrough battle. A Panzer 38 (t) tank lies damaged in the ditch, and an Sd.Kfz. 10/4 with an ammunition trailer has run afoul of 2-cm AA guns. Across the road a Russian scout car and several wrecks can be seen in the field. To the left, a "light towing tractor 3 t (Sd.Kfz. 11)" with the tactical symbol of a howitzer battery and a medium uniform personnel car are seen. All the vehicles bear air spotting markings – a necessary measure when the motorized units advanced quickly. (BA)

A Uniform Diesel beside a huge explosion crater into which one of the rare Belgian antitank guns, "Canon de 47 mm sur Vickers-Carden-Lloyd T.13", almost disappeared. (BA)

A broken-down Uniform Diesel of the 1st Mountain Division in Romania in 1941. A fuel truck with signs reading "Inflammable! Smoking and open lights forbidden!"

A field kitchen with 6-wheel drive: rear view of a Uniform Diesel with "large field cookstove Fkh. 13" distributing food.

Driving with a gas mask on – fortunately, this was never needed in World War II.

A factory-new "light off-road-capable truck, open, with uniform light truck chassis" on a test ride in 1938. The door lettering says: Net weight 4700 kg – Load limit 2425 kg or 25 persons –trailer limit 3500 kg – divide load evenly! (Photo: German Museum, Munich)

August 1941: A Uniform Diesel of the Mountain Jäger fords a stream in Estonia. It is towing a defective Kübelwagen (probably a Wanderer W 14) on a towing jack.

Panzer Group 3 (Hoth) advances in the summer of 1941. The supply units in their Uniform Diesels closely follow the tanks.

The "Survey and Equipment Truck (Kfz. 63" with uniform chassis for light trucks" was intended for a crew of 7 men plus driver and had an additional door to the rear area.

"Snow blower on Uniform Chassis", according to H.Dv. 471 (1939), with dual front wheels, rear door, halftracks and rear lights. On the rear are the air intake, radiator and coupling for the snow blower. The camouflage paint shown here surely was not the best for winter use.

Along with the open truck with open cab, there were a variety of closed bodies with closed cabs. The picture shows a "sound evaluation truck (Kfz. 62) with uniform chassis for light trucks" of Panzer Observation Battery 321 in readiness near Amapol on the Vistula on June 22, 1941. This vehicle, with license number WH-790516, bears number 11 on the front. The very low bottom transverse links, which limited ground clearance to 28 cm, are easy to see.

Two Kfz. 62 of Panzer Observation Battery 321 are stuck in the Ukrainian mud. At left is number 11 seen above (with the symbol of the 9th Panzer Division on the door), at right WH-632130, with number 24 and "K" for Panzer Group 1 on bumper and fender.

A Uniform Diesel with closed body on a corduroy road, which according to the caption was constantly maintained by the front workers of the Organization Todt. (BA)

Railroad transport of Kfz. 62 (WH-632130) of Panzer Observation Battery 321; at left, for comparison, is an open-bodied Uniform Diesel. The triangular box between the hind wheels held the tire chains. On flatbed trucks with angular rear fenders, these were housed in storage cases on the front edge.

Radio mast truck (Kfz. 68) on uniform chassis for light trucks" during extremely laborious and unpopular "preparation for inspection."

Here is another uniform truck that actually had the chassis of the light truck (one-ton load) but ran as a heavy personnel vehicle. The picture shows a particularly interesting example, a "telephone truck (Kfz. 23) with Uniform Chassis II for heavy personnel vehicles", with the typical third side door. Despite four-wheel drive and steering (note the angle of the rear wheels), this "heavy uniform personnel car" with a fighting weight of 4.5 tons apparently could only get over this hump in Bulgaria (spring 1941) by using every bit of its power.

FAUN-Werke, Nürnberg

The Fahrzeugfabriken Ansbach und Nürnberg AG (FAUN) came into being in 1919 from a merger of the "Fahrzeugfabriken Ansbach AG" and the "Nürnberger Feuerlöschgeräte-, Automobillastwagen- und Fahrzeugfabrik." The production program included trucks from 2 to 9 tons, with the numbers of each held within modest limits. FAUN received Wehrmacht contracts for, among others, the Uniform Diesel (700), the 9-ton truck (also as a tank transporter), and heavy wheeled tractors.

A requisitioned 5-ton FAUN on the Don Highroad in the summer of 1942. The clouds of dust were murderous for the motors – the vehicles simply were not intended for such extreme conditions.

Winter 1942-43: Near Staranya-Russa this FAUN L 900 (WL-282684) laboriously crawls up an icy slope, pulling a trailer. The vehicle had a load limit of nine tons and could be driven by 6- or 8-cylinder Deutz Diesel engines with 13.5 liters and 150 HP or 18 liters and 200 HP.

A rail-capable FAUN 9-ton Type L 900 of the 5th Co., Railway Engineer Regiment 3 in Rostov in August 1942, with a crane capable of lifting 7 to 9 tons. For (very laborious) conversion from road to rail use, all the wheels were removed and the rear axle, plus the "blind axle" under the cab, were fitted with railroad wheels. The sprung shock absorber can be seen at the front bumper.

Side view of the 9-ton FAUN with a crane that could lift 5 to 8 (maximum 10) tons. The "blind axle" behind the front wheels can be seen.

This 9-ton FAUN with its crane reinforced to lift ten tons, used by Landing Engineer Battalion 771, was set afire by Allied bombers near Kralyevica on 9/19/1944

Ford-Werke AG, Köln-Niehl

The "Ford Motor Company AG" founded for the German market went into business in Berlin in 1926, purely as an assembly plant. In 1931 it was moved to Köln-Niehl. As of 1935 its change into an independent German auto manufacturer was completed. The firm's name became "Ford-Werke AG" in 1939.

The most important Wehrmacht trucks were the various three-ton types (about 5000) and the halftrack "Maultier" truck (ca. 15,000).

The type letters and numbers, such as those of the G 398 TS, have the following meanings:

G = Germany
3 = model year 1943 (9 = 1939)
9 = 3.9-liter motor (1 = 3.6, 8 = 3.2 liters)
8 = model
T = truck
S = standard (4 x 2)

A 1942 advertisement: a Ford 3-ton V 3000 S truck (Type G 198 TS) seen on a military bridge in Russia.

Top: A 2.5-ton Ford Model BB of 1937 (4 cyl., 3.2 liters, 52 HP) passes a French Char B 1 bis tank.

Center: A Ford Model BB of 1937 of JG 53 with a broken axle in France in 1940.

Right: This Ford BB was still used by the 1st Mountain Division in 1943 but had to be destroyed during the retreat from Kerch. In the foreground is a container lettered "Glysantin Anti-Freeze, 50 liters, Army."

Small Truck Column 653 near Rouen on 10/11/1940, photographed by Propaganda Company 612. The picture shows a 3-ton 1939 Ford, the so-called Ford Uniform Truck, WH-265704.

This type, with its oval grille, was made in the USA since 1938 and produced in somewhat changed form in Germany since 1939. The typical feature of all Fords made in Germany was the undivided front bumper. The 3-ton truck had a 3.6-liter Ford V8 motor giving 90 HP (Type G 917 T St IIIa) or a 95 HP, 3.9-liter Ford V8 as G 997 T St IIIb. (BA)

Ford Type G 917 T or 997 T, here with an open cab, as a supply vehicle of a Luftwaffe unit.

Near Maikop in southern Russia in the summer of 1942: Ford Model V8-51 of the 5th Co., Railway Engineer Regiment 3, with open cab and single-axle trailer (possibly an air compressor). Behind it are a Büssing-NAG Type G 31 and a captured Russian truck. The V8-51 was built from 1937 to 1939 and had a 3.5-liter V8 gasoline motor producing 90 HP.

This requisitioned bus from the Düsseldorf district was used by the Bavarian 57th I.D. as a motorized dentist's office in Poland in the autumn of 1939. This vehicle used the Ford V8-51 chassis and the grille of the Ford V8 Special car.

Ford 3-ton 1939 model on the Russian steppes; note the headlight covers and the triangular symbol on the right fender.

This 3-ton 1939 Ford of a medical company of the 6th SS Mountain Division "Nord" was forced into a ditch near Nivalla in the autumn of 1942.

The constantly overstrained troops had many accidents attributable to exhaustion. The driver of this 1939 3-ton Ford (carrying fuel and equipment) of the 19th Panzer Division suddenly woke up in a roadside ditch near Roslavl in the autumn of 1941! The flat fender shape of the final version is easy to see here.

All Ford trucks could be modified to run on wood-gas for use back home. On the G 917 T (3.6-liter) and G 997 (3.9-liter) 8-cylinder types, the gas cooler (usually made by Imbert) was mounted in front of the radiator grille, the bars of which had to be cut off. On the G 987 T (3.2-liter) 4-cylinder type, the gas cooler was mounted under the motor hood. This picture shows a G 997 T in Wuppertal, with wood-gas system and Rhine Province registration with a "red chevron" (proof of permission for civilian vehicles). The gas generator (made by Imbert, 550 mm diameter) can be seen in the back, and under the bumper is the residue tank, the cleaning of which was an extremely unpleasant job.

Only a few were built: the ambulance (Kfz. 31) on Ford 3-ton chassis (with single rear wheels), made by the coachbuilding firm of Christian Miesen.

Made to the American pattern, but with undivided windshield, the new 3-ton Ford appeared in 1941 as Type G 198 TS (3.9-liter V8 gasoline motor). The Wehrmacht called it Type V 3000 S. The picture shows a Ford V 3000 S near Rshev in October 1942. A first-series vehicle, recognizable by the type letter S on the grille and "ornamentation to left and right" (with Ford monogram) on the rim of the motor hood. The number 17, the helmet emblem of the "Grossdeutschland" I.D. (mot.), and the tactical symbol for "large truck column for fuel (50 cubic meters) 1/13" are easy to see.

A convoy on the Kalmuck Steppes: A Panzer III tows a Ford V 3000 S of the 7th I.D., a Krupp covered truck and a car out of roadless terrain.

A 3-ton Ford with wood-gas drive in action with the Reich Work Service. The gas generator and fuel were kept between the cab and the rear body on the Ford Type G 188 TG (4 cylinders, 3.2 liters).

A Ford V 3000 S captured from the Americans, seen at Reims in 1944. This is a late version with flat fenders, short bumper, modified hood attachment and small primary headlights.

The Ford V 3000 S appeared in 1943 with a larger radiator as the G 388 TS (4 cylinders, 3.2 liters) and G 398 TS (V8, 3.9 liters). The vehicle had additional louvers at the front of the motor hood and two air intakes on top of the hood. The picture shows "one of the survivors" in Berlin shortly after the war ended.

Factory photo of a Ford V 3000 S (G 398 TS) with uniform cab, grille guard, high radiator, staff and towing eye on one side. The arrow on the grille indicates the built-in Winter Special Equipment 92.

In 1943-44, small numbers of an all-wheel drive, cabover version of the 3-ton truck were built. The American Ford COE of 1939 (COE = cab over engine) was its godfather. The picture comes from "Krafthand" of January 1945 and is entitled: "Supply trucks roll in long columns from our factories to all fronts."

This vehicle was designated Ford V 3000 A (G 198 TWA), which refers to a development of 1941. The "W" is not listed in the type code —it may mean "Wehrmacht." The truck had a V8, 3.9-liter, 95 HP gasoline engine and was used chiefly in Norway. The picture shows Finnish drivers shortly after the German retreat.

Henschel und Sohn GmbH, Kassel

The Henschel firm was already producing locomotives and railroad materials in the 19th century. As of 1928, trucks were also included in its production. By the end of the war, Henschel had produced a total of 25,035 trucks (including buses).

Special trucks for troop use included the Uniform Diesel (ca. 1500) and particularly the off-road 3-ton Type 33 D1 (gasoline) and Type 33 G1 (Diesel), of which (including Types B1 and FA1) 22,000 were built. (Note: according to other, likewise reliable sources, 10,300 were delivered; the rest may have been exported).

KHD built more than 3800 of the Type 33 G1 with their own Deutz motors.

Henschel advertisement from 1939.

73

HENSCHEL & SOHN GM BH KASSEL

Henschel quality: This Henschel Rex "medium fuel truck (o)" of 1926 was still in service at the Focke-Wulf factory airfield in Bremen in the autumn of 1940. Here it is fueling the Focke-Wulf Fw 190 with factory number 0022.

This Henschel 6 J 1, a 6.5-ton truck with 6-cylinder, 125 HP Diesel engine, broke down while being loaded on a train in Orscha in June 1944.

A 4-ton Henschel 40 S 2 on the road from Millerovo to the Don in the summer of 1942. The truck already had the new radiator grille, and had been built with a 6-cylinder, 95 HP Diesel engine since 1937.

The Henschel & Son Type 33 3-ton truck as medium AA gun truck (m.gl.Lkw. off.(o)), which served as a towing vehicle for the 3.7 cm Flak 18 gun and had as its crew a driver, an aide, a gun leader, seven gunners and two air sentries. On the frame behind the cab is the 5-ton winch, over it the case for the 25-meter (sometimes 50 meter), 14 mm towing cable with 15-ton strength. The two spare wheels were attached under the bed at the rear. (a = two guns in racks, c = long spade).

The same truck (WL-62338) from the right side. Under the cab are the large first-series compressed-air tanks for the brakes. Sometimes two tanks, one behind the other, were used, but most types had two transverse compressed-air tanks above the rear frame. On the sides are the tire chains in their racks, and the broken pieces of the bed are in front of the cab.

Driving school (off-road) at Grafenwöhr in March 1937. The (prewar) "lying double 7" symbol indicated Engineer Battalion 7 of Rosenheim. The Henschel Type 33 was built with various bumpers, this one the simple tube form of an early series. Note the U-shaped attachments for engineering equipment on the ends of the frame.

Most Henschel Type 33 trucks were used by the engineers. This truck (with double bumper) of Engineer Battalion 14 was pushed off the road and against a tree by the vehicle behind it in the spring of 1935.

A typical street scene near Orel: Feldjäger troops direct the traffic, and in front is a sign for the staff of the 5th Panzer Division, at right a Büssing-NAG, in the center a Henschel Type 33 with the rare flat steel bumper and centrally located camouflage headlight mounted on a pipe.

A Bridge Column B on the Autobahn: Henschel Type 33 as Engineer Truck 1 with Pontoon Truck (Pf. 11). The MG 34 gun, carried according to plan, is mounted on turning AA struts. Most trucks used by the grenadier and engineer companies were equipped with a "bottom hole for attaching the mount" in the bed, to be covered by a flap.

A Henschel Type 33 equipment truck of the railway engineers in Fordon, Poland.

A Henschel Type 33 with typical prewar camouflage paint.

A Henschel Type 33 from the Berlin district. All of the lights have camouflage covers – a camouflage light has not yet been installed. Note the eye of the winch cable under the left headlight; it ran through the fender (flap on the back).

A propaganda scene is being prepared! Though the damaged BF 109 E has a customary German cross in this picture, a second photo shows this white 14 still on the same single-axle carrier, but with a rosette! Who knows what was going on? Towing it is a Henschel Type 33.

Raw fodder for the horses, or for the troops to sleep on? Since this truck belonged to the 5th Panzer Division, as the symbol on the right fender indicates, the latter was quite possible. This Henschel Type 33 (WH-28855) does not show whether its camouflage headlight lit part of the "deer antlers", which was not at all what the installation instructions called for.

The trucks shown on this page were all special vehicles of the foglaying troops, on the chassis of the Henschel Type 33. They were rarely seen and usually used for other purposes. This picture shows a water tank truck (Kfz. 94). The vehicle could carry 2700 liters of water that could be warmed by a built-in heater and pumped to the detoxifying jets.

Clothing detoxifying truck (Kfz. 93), in which clothing could be cleaned of combat substances with steam and chemicals.

Personnel detoxifying truck (Kfz. 92b), in which contaminated personnel could get a thorough cleaning with warm water and chemicals.

A Henschel Type 33 with closed body and cab, as a telephone service truck (Kfz. 72). The two compressed-air tanks for the brake system are easy to see under the rear.

A tank pumper (Kfz. 343) of an airfield fire department, with a civilian "fireman" at the nozzle. The vehicle, a Henschel Type 33 D1 (or D 600), had a water capacity of 2500 liters and a four-man crew.

Klöckner-Humboldt-Deutz AG, Ulm Works (Magirus)

Magirus was already building military trucks during World War I. In 1935 the firm was absorbed into the Klöckner-Humboldt-Deutz undertaking; KHD built Diesel engines and tractors, Magirus built trucks.

The most important vehicles for the Wehrmacht were the Type M 206 (1150), the Uniform Diesel (2500), the Type 33 G1 (under license from Henschel, 3800), and the three-ton truck in A- or S-versions, some 16,000 to perhaps 20,000 were built. There were also 1750 of the tracked "Maultier" truck.

Many of the heavy Magirus trucks were developed and built as fire trucks.

The 3-ton Magirus Type M 30 (4 x 2) was built from 1931 to 1934 and had a 6-cylinder, 4.5-liter gasoline motor giving 70 HP. The picture shows an intelligence workshop truck of a unit from Bremen in the spring of 1940.

The three-axle Magirus M 206 (6 x 4) had the same Magirus S 88 motor as the Type M 30 and was built from 1934 to 1937. As a light off-road vehicle (o) it reached the troops with various bodies; this is the radio truck (Kfz. 61) of a Stuttgart intelligence unit.

A supply column of Panzer Group 1 (von Kleist) fords the Dniepr at Cherkassy in 1941. In front is a requisitioned 3-ton Magirus (M 25/M 27/M 30) built around 1935.

A Magirus M 206 as a light off-road vehicle (o). The horizontal cooling louvers are unusual.

Although large numbers of the 3-ton Magirus were built for the troops from 1941 to 1943, few action photos of this type are available. The truck existed in both A and S versions, the latter being shown here. Each had a Humboldt-Deutz Diesel engine (Type F 4 M 513, 4 cylinders, 4.9 liters, 80 HP). The precise designation according to D 666/8 of 1/28/1943 was "Lastkraftwagen 3 t Maguris Baumuster Klöckner S 3000/A 3000."

A 3-ton Magirus (S 3000 or A 3000) being towed by a light 1-ton towing tractor with a strikingly large cover, probably a self-propelled gun carriage (Sd.Kfz. 10.4) with a 2 cm Flak gun.

From 1942 to 1944, a halftrack truck, the "Maultier" (Mule), was built on the basis of the Magirus S 3000. Its type designation in D 666/407 (2/15/1943) was "Lkw 3 t mit Gleiskette (Maultier) Klöckner-Humboldt-Deutz A.G. Werk Ulm Baumuster S 3000/SSM." The picture was taken in the area of the 11th Panzer Division in the winter of 1943-44. On the grille, next to the left headlight, the hot water box with its locking lid can be seen; here a blow lamp could be used to warm the cooling water (Winter Kit No. 180).

Buses of the 7th I.D. in Poland: one Mercedes, one MAN and one 3-ton Magirus with the firm's emblem on the radiator cap.

A bus on the chassis of the 3-ton Magirus.

Only about 600 of the Magirus S 4500 (125 KP Diesel) were built.

In 1941, forty Magirus L 365 6-ton trucks (with Deutz Diesel engines, 6 cylinders, 13.5 liters, 145 HP) were rebuilt into rail trucks at the Reichsbahn works in Opladen.

A technical stop of an NSKK column, which was uniformly equipped with Magirus M 165 6.5-ton trucks. The front plate reads "NSKK Transporte Speer, Warning, Column."

Fried. Krupp AG, Essen

The "Abt. Kraftwagenfabrik" produced its first truck, a 5-ton type of its own design, in 1919. Until the war began, Krupp built a variety of high-performance trucks, generally with air-cooled motors of its own manufacture.

The 1.5-ton Krupp-Protze and the 3-ton L 3 H 63.163 were developed especially for military use.

Taking the LD 2 H 142 as an example, the code is:
L = Lastwagen (truck)
D = Diesel motor
2 = load (2 tons)
H = Hochrahmen (high frame)
1 = first modification
4 = four-cylinder
2 = two-axle

The progenitor of the 1.5-ton Krupp (6 x 4) truck was the "light off-road vehicle with air-cooled 60-HP carbureted motor (L 2 H 43) or 50-HP Diesel motor (LD 2 H 43)." Its motor hood had not yet taken on the typical sloped form.

The Krupp Protze (Kfz. 69) L 2 H 43 during winter maneuvers. The 143 version had, among other things, longer bumpers than the 43 type and a motor (Krupp M 304, 4 cylinders, gasoline, 3.3 liters) boosted from 55 to 60 HP.

The Krupp L 2 H 143 personnel truck (Kfz. 70) of MG Battalion 6 of Coburg. The truck in front features several technical differences from the others: higher winch and spotlight mounts, different direction-indicator attachment, added wind deflectors and greater distance between the windshield and motor hood.

Flanders, 1940: A "Light Searchlight Truck I (Kfz. 83 with chassis of the light off-road Lkw. (o)", a Krupp L 2 H 143. In the rear is the 8-kilowatt generator for the anti-aircraft searchlight on the trailer. Note the asymmetrical cylinder covering of the air-cooled opposed motor between the hood and fenders. The truck belonged to the "General Goering" Regiment.

A Krupp L 2 H 43 of a Stuttgart unit, used as a "practice tank."

Two Krupp L 2 H 143 personnel trucks (Kfz. 70) with certain detail modifications (windshield, rear sides, etc.), as the alert observer can see.

The Krupp 1.5-ton truck was usually used as a limber for towing the 3.7 cm Pak gun. Hence the common name of "Krupp-Protze" for these trucks.

A Krupp L 2 H 143 limber (Kfz. 69) driving onto an engineer bridge in France in 1940. Note the barrage-wire holder added by some units; it could also be used to carry a "liberated" bicycle. (BA)

Tank battle near Juvigny, June 6-7, 1940: The Krupp Protze of Mountain Panzerjäger Unit 44 (1st Mountain Division) with its small 3.7 cm Pak gun remains in readiness while an 8-ton towing tractor thunders by, bringing an 8.8 cm AA gun up for antitank use. The difference in size is really striking!

A limber rebuilt by the troops, carrying a 3.7 cm Pak gun of Mountain Panzerjäger Unit 44, on the banks of the Marne near Chateau Thierry on June 12, 1940. Note the shaped steel design with the attached wheel hub, the spar carried on the side, and the attachment for the gun wheels at the rear.

In the spring of 1941, Mountain Panzerjäger Unit 44 used several Krupp L 2 H 43 trucks with fully turning 3.7 cm Pak guns installed.

Under the direction of Lt. Kaiser, two Krupp Protze (Sf.) trucks were fitted with 8 mm front armor (made by Skoda) and, as this picture shows, used successfully at the beginning of the Russian campaign. The box of ammunition on the back can be seen, as can the two seats for the rear gun crew. Both "assault guns" were destroyed by Russian antitank fire in the autumn of 1941.

"Medium off-road Lkw. (o) Krupp L 3 H 163" of the 5th SS Panzer Division "Viking" on the Danube bridge at Nikopol, Bulgaria. The 3-ton (6 x 4) truck had a 6-cylinder, 7.5-liter gasoline motor producing 110 HP. (BA)

At the Polish-Russian border on 6/13/1941: a Krupp L 3 H 163 of the 5th Co., Railway Engineer Regiment 3, with wide shield for an MG 34 in the back.

Krupp L 3 H 163 of an unidentified Luftwaffe unit a "medium off-road Lkw. open (o)" with (atypically) closed cab.

Only two radiator sections in the bashed nose of this Krupp L 3 H 163 survived an accident in the Smolensk area in 1941. As usual for vehicles of A.R. 29 (mot.), it carried not the eagle of the 29th I.D. (mot.) but a big diamond on the left fender. The collapsible canvas fuel container was part of its equipment.

A Krupp L 3 H 163 at the Grafenwöhr driving school in March 1937. Note the Krupp name on the grille, the "antlers" ahead of the grille, and the telephone-cable racks on the fenders. The "F" shows it to be a telephone truck.

An interesting foglaying-troop vehicle, a Krupp L 3 H 163 with double cab, to transport the 10 cm Fog Launcher 35 and its crew, consisting of the launcher leader and six men. (WH-101 232).

The Krupp L 3 H 63 as Flamethrower Truck I (Kfz. 74) with the chassis of the medium off-road Lkw (o). The truck was designed for driver, aide, and 12-man crew. Unlike the 163 version, Type 63 had louvers instead of vent flaps on the motor hood.

The Krupp L 3 H 163 with box body as a photography truck (Kfz. 354) of the Luftwaffe.

The Krupp L 3 H 163 with airfield searchlights made by the Siemens-Schuckert Works, plus a built-in generator.

A Krupp L 3 H 163 made into a mobile operating room for the 1st Medical Company of the "Grossdeutschland" Panzer Corps, seen during the withdrawal to the Dniestr in February or March of 1944.

A requisitioned Krupp LD 3.5 M 222 with M 402 Diesel engine (60 HP) or Krupp L 3.5 M 242 with M 202 gasoline engine (75 HP).

A two- or three-ton Krupp truck with Westphalian registration. Krupp produced a great number of types, and it is not always possible to identify them precisely.

Draft and pack horses of the 1st Mountain Division transported on a Krupp LD 6.5 N 242 with 125 HP Diesel engine (Junkers license) of Truck Transport Regiment 616, heading for Lyon on June 23, 1940. At right is a Phänomen Granit in rare Kübelwagen form.

This Krupp OD 4 N 232 bus was shot up in Brussels in August 1944. The vehicle had a 90 HP Diesel engine, built under license by Junkers, thus the symbol of the "flying man" over the Krupp rings.

Maschinenfabrik Augsburg-Nürnberg AG (MAN), Nürnberg

The MAN firm began to produce trucks in 1915, building Saurer vehicles under license.

The most important types made for the Wehrmacht were: 1. the 3-ton Type E 3000 (also built by Fross-Büssing in Vienna), some 3000 of which were built, 2. the 4.5-ton Type ML 4500 in S- and A- versions (built under license by ÖAF in Vienna), of which there were about 10,000, 3. the 6.5-ton Type F4 (built under license by Fross-Büssing), with 2500 built, and 4. the Uniform Diesel, with 1800 built.

Advertisement for the MAN Type ML 4500 S. This 4.5-ton truck was very popular among the troops, particularly in all-wheel-drive ML 4500 A form. The truck had an MAN Diesel engine, Type D 1040 G, with 6 cylinders, 7.9 liters, 110 HP, and was built from 1940 until the end of the war.

A factory photo of the MAN Type ML 4500 A light Lkw (o) made in 1941. The registration is from Nürnberg, the red chevron on the license plate was the prized proof of permission for civilian use.

A bogged-down fuel tanker of an SS tank unit in the Ukraine, an MAN Type ML 4500.

Munich, autumn 1945: The final version of the MAN Type ML 4500 A still looked quite passable, compared to many other products.

This MAN Type ML 4500 S fights its way through the mud (4/28/1942). The S version is recognizable by the lack of reduction gears (in front), the depression in the middle of the front wheel, and the louvers of different lengths, which can be seen here under the spade. (BA)

"Heaviest Truck", the MAN Type F 4 was called in the firm's advertising. Under the massive motor hood was either a 6-cylinder, 13.3-liter, 150 HP Diesel or a 12.2-liter type giving 120 HP. The load limit was 6.5 to 8 tons. This picture shows a (requisitioned) supply truck of a subordinate division before the Army supply depot in Heinsberg near Wesel on 2/23/1940. (BA)

"Wheels must roll for victory": According to this propaganda slogan, even this old 3-ton MAN Type Z (6-cylinder Diesel, 60 HP) of the 1st Mountain Division was sent off in the direction of Uman.

The 3-ton MAN Type E 3000 (4 x 2, 6-cylinder Diesel, 70 HP) was built only in small numbers.

A requisitioned MAN Type E 3000 medium Lkw. (o) of an intelligence unit.

"The Schongauer" in Poland in 1939. This bus on the chassis of the MAN Type E 2 was given a very colorful camouflage paint job by the 57th I.D.

Adam Opel AG, Rüsselsheim and Brandenburg

The Opel works began to build trucks in 1919 and produced 3-and 4-ton models in World War I. After financial difficulties in the twenties, General Motors acquired all the stock of the Opel firm between 1928 and 1931. In 1931, production of the 1.5- and 3-ton Opel Blitz truck to American standards began. These vehicles' advantages included a high load limit with low net weight, solid workmanship and a reliable Buick motor.

Over 95,000 of the standard Blitz-S was built, and it was rated as off-road capable. A better off-road version, the Blitz-A with all-wheel drive, appeared in 1940; 25,000 of them were built, and they were found very satisfactory by the troops. 3500 Blitz trucks were built under license by Daimler-Benz. Planned construction by Borgward did not take place on account of the war situation. Some 4000 of the tracked "Maultier" truck were also delivered.

A 2.5-ton Opel Blitz (built until 1935) of the Legion Condor as an ambulance.

A Luftwaffe ambulance on the Opel Blitz 1.5-ton chassis. Dual rear wheels, as seen on this vehicle, were not at all common on ambulances.

A rather old-fashioned Opel Type 10/45 of 1930 (1.5-ton load, 45 HP gasoline motor) as a light truck of a medical unit (or perhaps Technische Nothilfe).

"New-Type Assault Gun": a 2.5-ton Opel Blitz (first built in 1935) loaded with a 3.7 cm Pak gun during a prewar maneuver.

A 1-ton Opel Blitz used as a limber for a 3.7 cm Pak gun.

The 1-ton Opel Blitz had a 6-cylinder, 2-liter, 36 HP gasoline motor and was first built in 1934. This requisitioned panel truck was used as a radio van.

The sturdy chassis of the Opel Blitz was very well suited to use with bus bodies. This Luftwaffe bus used the chassis of the 2.5-ton Opel Blitz of 1935.

A 1.5-ton Opel Blitz of the Wilhelmshaven motor vehicle unit was used as a personnel vehicle in August 1940.

The best-known German truck was surely the 1937 3-ton Opel Blitz (4 x 2) 3.6-36 S. It had a straight 6-cylinder, 3.6-liter Opel gasoline engine, producing 75 HP (detuned to 68 HP) and was built until August 1944. In July 1940 an all-wheel-drive version of the 3-ton truck appeared, to enjoy the greatest popularity among the troops because of its off-road capability, reliability and, above all, excellently organized spare-parts supply. This "Lkw 3 t Opel 6700 Type A" had the same motor as the S version, and all essential components were interchangeable. According to D 666/5 (7/1/1942) there were the following standard body types:

1. 600 mm high box van with transverse seats and extending boards
2. Open box with two built-in longitudinal seat benches.
3. Closed box body.

The Opel Blitz S type (above) can be told from the A type (below) by the following features, among others:

1. The front reduction gears of the A type
2. Straight lower rim of the upper side panel of the motor hood of the A type
3. Less distance between the front fenders and doors of the A type
4. Different front wheels.

South Russia, summer 1942: An Opel Blitz 3 t Type S with unusual cab and the tactical symbol of a field hospital (mot.), followed by a 1.5-ton 1938 Chevrolet and a 2-ton Peugeot Type DMA. (BA)

This 3-ton Opel Blitz Type S – obviously a repair-shop truck with lengthened bed and "dachshund's belly" for tools and equipment –surely can no longer be called off-road capable. The load is a corduroy road, as was made by the troops out of wood and wire.

A 3-ton Opel Blitz S of Landing Engineer Battalion 86 in the Strumica-Strip area, autumn 1944. A late version with refined grille, the small headlights of the last war years, simplified steps, no rear fenders and no triangular trailer symbol.

The 3-ton Opel Blitz S was certainly versatile, but not amphibious!

Engineers of Engineer Battalion 18 (mot.) prepare roads and bridges for the attack across the Niemen near Merkine on June 22, 1941. The 18th I.D. (mot.) had been equipped chiefly with French trucks, and had only a few 3-ton Opel Blitz trucks (here Type S with high box) in action. The cycle messenger wears an armband with the emblem of the 18th I.D. (mot.) and the lettering "traffic control."

Opel Blitz 3-ton Type S with KG 77 in East Prussia in the autumn of 1939. The squadron was still using Do 17 Z planes at that time.

Rail transport for a 3-ton Opel Blitz S with carefully attached wheels and lashings. The "Comrades of the Luftwaffe" where comfortable slippers over their colorful service socks. Note the slits of the headlights – and the lack of a camouflage light. The second truck may be a British Commer.

The repair-shop platoon of the Truck Unit of Wilhelmshaven, equipped with 3-ton Opel Blitz trucks.

Peenemünde, Test Pad I, August 1, 1943: Preparations for the launch of an A 4 (V-2) long-distance rocket. According to "Procedure Instructions (secret), Special Vehicles, Components and Essential Parts of Ground Facilities FR (no date)", the trucks and trailers of rocket batteries were not given Kfz., Sd.Kfz. or Ah. numbers, but rather "Fahrzeug-Pos." numbers. The rocket stands on the "Launching Platform (Fz.-Pos.-Nr. 103), erected by "F.R. Trailer (s) (3-axle)(Fz.-Pos.-Nr. 102)", with "A-Stoff Trailer 6 (2-axle)(Fz.-Pos.-Nr. 402)" behind it, pulled by a Hanomag SS 100. At the left front is an Opel Blitz 3-ton Type S with open cab (customary for tankers) as "Tank Truck 3500 l B-Stoff (Fz.-Pos.-Nr. 404), at right an Opel Blitz 3-ton Type A as "Tank Truck 2100 l T-Stoff (Fz.-Pos.-Nr. 405)."

It speaks well of the Opel Blitz's reliability that the F.R. batteries were equipped almost exclusively with these trucks. This is the Opel Blitz 3-ton Type S as "Tank Truck 2100 l T-Stoff (Fz.-Pos.-Nr. 405)"; "T-Stoff" was hydrogen peroxide. (Photo: German Museum, Munich) 1. Cab door, 2. Front and rear coverings, 3. Holder, 4. T-Stoff tank, 5. Tank Cap Cover, 6. Tank Holder, 7. Double rear doors, 8. Trailer hitch, 9. Hand pump for tank, 10. Coupling, 11. Control lever, 12. Overflow pipe.

Opel Blitz 3 ton Type S as "Tank Truck 3500 l B-Stoff (Fz.-Pos.-Nr. 404)"; "B-Stoff" was mixed spirit and water. Note demonstration rear wheels, small headlights and arrow pointing to built-in winter equipment. (Photo: German Museum, Munich). 1. Tool chest, 2. Armature space (pumps, hoses), 3. Camouflage attachment, 4. Tubular ladder, 5. Cap cover with attachments.

Opel Blitz 3-ton Type A as "Lkw. 3 t closed (305) BS-Anlage 2" for supervision and guidance of V-2 ignition. The "305" comes from Kfz. 305 (m.Lkw.(o) with closed uniform body). (Photo: German Museum, Munich)

Opel Blitz 3-ton Type A as "Lkw 3 t closed (305) for Rocket Spare Parts." (Photo: German Museum, Munich)

A kitchen truck with box body loaded on a train, an Opel Blitz 3-ton Type S with Russian kitchen personnel and one soldier in a reversible winter uniform, which was introduced in 1943.

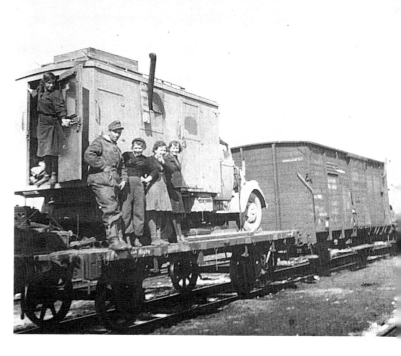

As of October 1942, Opel built some 4000 halftrack "Maultier" vehicles based on the Blitz S, almost all of them with open bodies. Here is a photo of the rare Opel "Maultier" with box body. The vehicle was used by the rocket batteries as "Lkw. 3 t closed (Maultier) LS Device Truck", "LS" standing for "Leitstrahl" (localizer beam). The wheel cutout remained and was fitted with a door so the space could be used for storage. Note the increase in allowable load to 3 tons in the last war years! (Photo: German Museum, Munich) 1. Jacks, 2. Cable openings, 3. Energy cable plug.

Phänomen, Zittau

The "Phänomen-Fahrradwerke Gustav Hiller AG" built its first truck, a 1.5-ton model called the Granit 25, in 1931. During the war, the factory built exclusively light trucks with air-cooled motors, which were used chiefly as ambulances.

"Ambulance (Kfz. 31) with chassis of the light truck (o)", a 1.5-ton (4 x 2) Phänomen Granit truck. This vehicle, of Ambulance Platoon 54 (1st Mountain Division), received shell damage in the rear near Rostov in 1942, splinters killing two patients. Note the first-series cab without doors.

Phänomen Granit 25 H as Kfz. 31 with the customary closed cab. The white background of the red cross has been painted over for camouflage purposes.

Phänomen Granit 25 H Ambulance (Kfz. 31, WH-12280) with the tactical symbol of an ambulance platoon and the emblem of the 61st Infantry Division. This vehicle had an air-cooled 4-cylinder 2.5-liter gasoline engine that produced 37 HP.

The Phänomen Granit 25 H ambulance had fully insufficient interior heating; only a small "radiation heater" was supplied, through which the driver could conduct exhaust gas by moving a lever. For Russian winter use, this was naturally not enough, especially when the vehicles were in traffic jams or had not been warmed up. The picture shows a vehicle of the 3rd SS Panzer Division "Totenkopf" in the area south of Lake Ilmen (1941-42); an open fire has been built under the vehicle to raise the temperature a bit for the patients.

The Phanomen Granit 30 had a 55 HP motor and a load limit of 2.3 tons. Only a few examples reached the Wehrmacht. This is an ambulance (Kfz. 31) of the Luftwaffe loading medical supplies into a Do 26.

The successor to the Type 25 H was the "Lkw. 1.5 t Phänomen Type Granit 1500 S (shown here) and A", built since 1940 and still built until 1956 by the IFA firm in the DDR. The Type A, which was very rare, could be recognized by the greater number of lugs on the front wheels and the single rear wheels.

The Phänomen Granit 1500 S at the Kuban bridgehead during the retreat of the 1st Mountain Division.

The red cross symbol did not prevent fighter-bombers of East or West from making low-level attacks. Here is a shot-up Phänomen Granit 1500 S ambulance near Arnheim in 1944. (BA)

Vogtländische Maschinenfabrik AG (Vomag), Plauen

Vomag produced a variety of small series of trucks, with loads of 3 to 9 tons, from 1915 to 1942. Special trucks for the Wehrmacht were not developed, but Vomag is said to have been involved in building an unknown number of Uniform Diesels.

Vomag 5-ton Type 5L truck, Vomag 4 R 3080 with Diesel engine, 4 cylinders, 9.5 liters, 100 HP.

Vomag 6-ton Type 6L truck, Vomag 6 R 3080 with Diesel engine, 6 cylinders, 14.3 liters, 150 HP. Requisitioned Vomag trucks were used almost exclusively by the motor transport regiments.

In the 1st Unit of Flak Regiment 42 (mot. S.), about 20 examples of an interesting vehicle came into being: the Vomag 9-ton low-floor truck (with bus chassis), used as a gun, survey or command equipment truck. This picture shows a gun truck with 8.8 cm Flak gun near Magdeburg in July 1941.

The same type of vehicle on its way to the Brussels area in the spring of 1942.

Captured Trucks and Products of Occupied Countries

The German troops captured many thousands of trucks from various countries, especially while they were on the advance. Unfortunately, statistics are not available – for one thing, because the records of the collecting places are no longer available, and for another, because many units never officially reported their "well-earned booty." During the war, the motor vehicle factories of the occupied countries produced goodly quantities of trucks for the Wehrmacht. Definite production figures of these firms are unnecessarily kept under lock and key to this day.

According to the war diary of Generaloberst Halder (Chief of the Army General Staff), the tense situation of the German motor vehicle industry made it necessary that, in the reorganization and establishment of "fast units" (Schnellen Verbänden)in April 1941, almost exclusively French material had to be used – and in the 20th P.D. as well as the 14th, 18th, 25th and 36th I.D. (mot.).

Without the many foreign vehicles, the large-scale German operations in World War II surely would have been impossible.

Packard

This photo of 56th I.D. vehicles in transport toward Kovel on the Bug in the summer of 1941 clearly shows the necessary confusion of truck types used by many German units: GMC T16B (4 x 4) of 1938 with "Belgian Army cabin"; Citroen 23; Chevrolet; Berliet; Uniform Diesel; Henschel, and various other makes.

"Bakery Company (mot.) come to assembly" at Höxter, March 12, 1940: a bus body (by Bauer) on the chassis of the 3-ton Austro-Fiat (ÖAF) Austor-Fiat (ÖAF) 5-ton Type FD6; and several Ford V8-51's. (BA)

Bakery Company (mot.) on the march, March 1940. In the foreground is a 5-ton Austro-Fiat (ÖAF) with Large Cookstove 13, still with an Austrian Army registration number.

A truck column of the Organization Todt on the march to Belgium. In front is an "Österreichische-Automobil-Fabriks-AG" (ÖAF) ex-Austro-Fiat 5-ton Type FD6 with 100 HP Diesel engine (MAN license). The lettering on the sign means "Chief Quartermaster Belgium."

Vehicles of the 1st Mountain Division on the autobahn near Munich. In front is an Austro-Daimler ADGR (3 tons, 6 x 4, 72 HP), behind it a Ford V8-51.

Some 3800 of the Steyr 640 (1.5 tons, 6 x 4, 55 HP) were built by 1941, particularly with ambulance bodies.

The 1.5-ton Steyr 640 trucks of S.R. 73 withdraw from Poland.

The "Lkw. 1.5 t Steyr Model 1500 A" was very popular among the troops because of its all-wheel drive, air-cooled V8 motor (85 HP) and sturdiness. Some 19,000 of them, mostly personnel vehicles (Kfz. 70), were built by the Steyr-Daimler-Puch A.G. in Steyr and the Auto-Union A.G. works in Siegmar. This picture shows a Model 1500 A/01 (covered spare wheel) of Flak Battalion 22 in the southern sector in 1942, followed by a "light 1-ton towing tractor with 2 cm Flak 38."

Withdrawal of the 1st Medical Company of "GD" to the Bug in the spring of 1944. The picture shows a Steyr Model 1500 A/02 (open spare wheel), a VW Kübel, and a 4.5-ton Büssing-NAG.

A group of Panzerjagdkommandos are shown here in a Steyr Model 1500A. Note the two Panzerfaust 30's just to the left of the open door.

Toward the end of the war, the Steyr 1500 A was classified as a two-ton vehicle, though whether it was then designated Steyr 2000 A (as listed in English sources) remains unproved. This is an "Electric Service Car on Lkw 2 t (Steyr), Vehicle-Pos.-Nr. 105" of the rocket troops (WH-1586286), seen in August 1944. The vehicle had a 6 KVA generator with Zündapp motor, direct-current transformer, batteries, switching station and five cable drums. Its job was providing power for all tests and switching checks before the launch of a V-2, so that the "on-board battery of the special device" would not be weakened. In the switching station, all the switches and testing devices worked together. It could tow a cable-drum trailer (Fahrzeug-Pos.-Nr. 110) with 8 cable drums. 1 = generator starter hatch, 2 = wheel for cable-layer. (Photo: German Museum, Munich)

The Czech Skoda H (6 x 4) had a load limit of 4 tons and a 6-cylinder, 8.2-liter gasoline engine with 100 HP. This Skoda (still with Czech registration above) was driven by Georg Birkmeyer in the French campaign as a tool delivery truck of the 212th I.D. (repair-shop company). On the door are "Z 2" and a (blue) shepherd with two sheep, symbol of the company leader, Oberleutnant Schäfer.

This Skoda H takes an upgrade beyond Rossoch (Don area). The vehicles probably belong to the 3rd Panzer Division, in action during "Operation Blue", 6/28-7/4/1942.

A Skoda H in Belgium in 1940.

This Tatra T 27 (3 tons, 4 x 2, 60 HP) is seen in the Weser-Flugzeugbau GmbH yards during the war.

At least 220 of the Tatra T 85 (5 tons, 6 x 4, 80 HP) were built as fuel tankers and generally used by the Luftwaffe. This is a Kfz. 384 fueling an Fw 190 of I./JG 54.

RINGHOFFER TATRA-WERKE
A. G. PRAG-SMICHOW

Advertisement of May 1942 for the 6.5-ton Tatra T 81 H (6 x 4, V-8 motor, 14.7 liters), which still produced some 150 HP with wood-gas drive.

A Luftwaffe column with three Tatra T 92 (2 tons, 6 x 4, 70 HP) trucks and one Tatra T 23.

"Whoever loves his vehicle, pushes." This cover picture of the NSKK periodical "Deutsche Kraftfahrt" of October 1942 shows a Tatra T 27 of the Organization Todt with civilian registration.

RAD workers pushing two Praga RN (3 tons, 4 x 2, 75 HP) trucks. This type was built from 1934-1953, which attests to its quality. Note the RAD license plate, not included in official lists.

Dunkerque was a treasure-house of high-quality British vehicles captured in June 1940.

This is how the roads around Dunkerque looked: British and French vehicles of all kinds and in every condition. The "Technical NSKK Battalion" salvaged 6500 vehicles in the Dunkerque area, according to contemporary reports, and was able to put 4500 of them into service. The rest were scrapped or turned over to the "Army Scrapping Command." Special recognition was accorded to the "NSKK Transportstandarte Todt Staffel Dünkirchen." The picture shows a Morris Commercial CD (6 x 4) beside a Somua halftrack.

A captured Albion BY 1 (3 tons, 6 x 4, 64 HP) is taken posses- sion of by the Motor Vehicle Unit of Wilhelmshaven.

Albion BY 1 in the 5th Echelon of JG 52.

Some 17,000 of the Austin K 3 (3 tons, 4 x 2, 60 HP) were built from 1939-1945. The picture shows a truck of the 216th I.D. in Kovno.

The newly formed A.R. 29 (mot.) underway from France to Italy in June 1943. In the center is an Austin K 3.

4600 of the Austin K 30 (4 tons, 4 x 2, 60 HP) were built. This is a burned-out ambulance of the 1st Mountain Division; the stretcher racks can still be seen clearly.

A Bedford OXD (2 tons, 4 x 2, 72 HP) captured by I.R. 398.

An O.T. unit crawls through the White Russian terrain (Minsk area, spring 1943), led by an STZ-5, followed by a GAZ-AAA, a Bedford MWD and an Opel Super 6. (BA)

During the war, Vauxhall Motors produced the impressive quantity of 66,000 Bedford MWD trucks (0.8 tons, 4 x 2, 72 HP). This picture shows a captured truck of the Luftwaffe, with a 3-ton Bedford OYD in the background.

Bedford MWD with an interesting body, about which no information is available.

Two Bedford MWD of Mountain Panzerjäger Unit 44 with camouflage headlights in Cilli, Yugoslavia. Here the "Cilli Death March", in which hundreds of German prisoners died, began in 1945.

Zymlianskaya, August 1942: On the arid steppes of the Don, this water-tank truck was of incalculable value. This Bedford MW "water dowser" was used by a unit with the designation 3./805 (Schweinfurt).

The Bedford OYD (4 x 2, 72 HP) was Britain's most often-built 3-ton truck (72,000 were built). The picture shows an early model (with dual rear wheels) with an MG 34 on a Tripod 34, guarding Belgian prisoners. The photo comes from an album of N.A. 27.

A Crossley JGL 8 (3 tons, 6 x 4, 75 HP) with crane, used by JG 2 on the Channel coast during the Battle of Britain.

Despite difficulty in obtaining spare parts, this Morris Commercial CVS 11/40 was still running in the Kiev area in the autumn of 1943 – surely a sign of good British quality and resourceful German mechanics.

A used-car show in Dunkerque in 1940. At right is a Guy PE (3 tons, 4 x 2, 55 HP), in the center a Morris Commercial 15 cwt, at left perhaps a Latil.

A heavily armed Morris Commercial 15 cwt (0.8 tons, 4 x 2, 60 HP) of the 35th I.D. stirring up propaganda dust.

The sign (left) at the Wehrmacht filling station in Veurne (NW Belgium) read: Army Filling Station Veurne. It is forbidden to get gas without 1. a valid order, 2. logbook, 3. permit. This must be entered in the logbook. The Local Commander." In the picture, a Morris Commercial 15 cwt fuel tanker (WH-558644) is being filled.

On June 10 and 11, 1942, the 3rd Co., Engineer Battalion 659 (mot.) had the task, along with Panzer Unit 202 (captured French tanks) of removing 24 barricades defended by partisans along the road from Bosanski Novi to Prijedor, Bosnia. Here a Morris Commercial of this unit drives along the Sana.

Mountain Jägers in North Africa! Special Unit 288 was chosen to fight in the mountains of the Near East as part of the "Orient Corps" and mount a pincer attack on the Suez Canal from the east. This did not happen, and so these mountain fighters were attached to the "Sperrverband Daumiller", which had the task of securing the open right flank of the Afrika-Korps on their withdrawal from Agedabia (December 1941). The picture shows the Company Leader, Lt. Werner Kost, in a captured Morris Commercial 15 cwt truck, with MG 34 on Tripod 34.

Scammell Pioneer R 100 (artillery tractor, 6 x 4, 102 HP) used by the 1st Naval Vehicle Unit in southern Russia, spring 1942. 768 of these vehicles were built, beginning in 1937.

The enormous numbers of vehicles produced in Canada are largely unknown to the Germans. By the end of the war, no fewer than 850,000 wheeled vehicles of all kinds had been built there. The CMP (Canadian Military Pattern) standardization reached a standard there that could only be dreamed of in Germany. The Canadian trucks may not have been much to look at, but their quality and durability were outstanding. The picture shows a captured Chevrolet C 60 (3 tons, 4 x 4, 85 HP) as a gun carrier.

Ford and Chevrolet built 209,000 Canadian 3-ton trucks, which had different motors, gearboxes and rear axles, but most of their other components were interchangeable. The main visible difference was the grille pattern, the Ford's square, the Chevrolet's weblike –as shown here. The C 60 could tow a 15 cm heavy Field Howitzer 18.

A French truck built by Bernard with fodder for the pack animals of the 1st Mountain Division. Note the man at left with spurs on his boots.

A 6-ton Berliet tanker (built in 1939) with 5000-liter tank, used by the 1st Panzer Division.

A Berliet 5-ton truck of the Light Assault Boat Command 902 in eastern Poland on July 22, 1941.

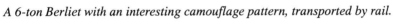

A 6-ton Berliet with an interesting camouflage pattern, transported by rail.

Two Citroen trucks of I.R. 51 in the area south of Lake Ilmen; at right a Citroen 23 U, at left a Citroen 11. The letter V and stripe of the 18th I.D. (mot.), called "rations canceled" by the soldiers, is easy to see.

Some 15,000 of the Citroen T 45 (3.5 tons, 4 x 2, 73 HP) were built for the Wehrmacht from 1941 to 1944. This is the commissary truck of a naval kitchen in Le Havre. The "MBK" lettering stands for "Naval Commander, Channel Coast."

The Citroen T 45 was also produced in series with a wood-gas generator. Here such a truck is seen after the war, scrounging in Upper Bavaria (B/Y 102 929).

The Matford F 917 WS (5 tons, 4 x 2, 85 HP) was built in great numbers for the Wehrmacht. Its quality and durability were criticized by the troops. The picture shows a truck of the 2nd Co., Engineer Battalion 3 (mot.), which was defeated at Stalingrad.

This captured French towing tractor (seen near St, Omer in 1940) would still be a prize for any technical museum today: a Latil TL artillery tractor, built about 1934, with 4-wheel drive and steering, 40 HP, extending off-road grippers, towing an acoustic aircraft locating device, such as was displayed in the Henriquez Collection near Trieste. (BA)

A captured Panhard K (5 tons, 4 x 2, 85 HP) with registration WH-680940, of an unidentified unit.

Mountain Jäger Regiment 756 arrived in Tunisia on January 6, 1943. The unit's trucks were to follow by ship but never arrived: Peugeot Type DMA (2 tons, 4 x 2, 50 HP), of which more than 15,000 were built for the Wehrmacht. This type of truck is recognizable chiefly by the projecting cab doors, an external sign of their strongly criticized quality of workmanship.

Some 14,000 of the Peugeot DK 5 light truck (1.4 tons, 4 x 2, 45 HP) were built for the Wehrmacht, with either open or closed bodies. The picture shows a Waffen-SS truck at Soignies on 9/3/1944.

A Peugeot DK 5 without a license plate in Belgium. The attachment of the headlight behind the grille was typical of Peugeot but very disadvantageous for night use.

A Peugeot DK 5 with closed body as an ambulance of the 1st Mountain Division. To avoid reflected light from the grilles, they have been removed.

The repair-shop truck of the 3rd Co., Bicycle Battalion 402, a captured Renault AGK (6 tons, 4 x 2, 85 HP) with a field post number as provisional registration.

This truck (SS-109625) of the 5th SS Panzer Regiment "Viking" was wrecked during a transfer from Wildflecken to Sennelager in May of 1942. It is a Renault AHN (3.5 tons, 4 x 2, 75 HP) that was built in large numbers for the Wehrmacht.

On guard in Dniepro, 1942. The Renault AHN (3.5 tons, 4 x 2, 75 HP) and Renault AHR (5-ton, 4 x 2, 75 HP) had the same type of cab and can be told apart only by the number of hoops (AHN had 6, AHR 7).

France built a variety of cabover trucks. This is a Renault, type unknown, at the driving school of the 57th I.D. on a practice run near Landshut in April 1941.

Renault AGR (4.5 tons, 4 x 2, 65 HP) with the tactical symbol of a motorized reconnaissance unit.

In the last years of the war, massive low-level air attacks in the east and west took a heavy toll of the usually fully unprotected supply columns. This picture shows a shot-up medical unit in Holland in 1944; at left a Renault AHN (AHR), at right a Renault AFB, which was intended to carry three patients. Remarkably, toward the end of the war many captured vehicles were used with their original license plates, with only a WH marking on the fender.

Unfortunately, no information is available on this interesting 2-ton Renault ADK with armored body.

Even this rebuilt Renault Paris bus had to see service with the 57th Infantry Division.

The Polish Polski Fiat 621 L (Fiat license) was built since 1931, with 12,600 built in all. The 4 x 2 vehicle had a load limit of 2.5 to 3 tons and a 50 HP motor. Photos of its use by the Wehrmacht, as here, are comparatively rare.

The Russian motor vehicle industry built its trucks almost exclusively under American Ford and Autocar licenses of the early thirties. The vehicles thus were technically obsolete but sturdy and easy to repair. In this picture, a GAZ-AA (1.5 tons, 4 x 2, 40 HP) of Engineer Battalion 260 is acquiring a closed body for field use.

The GAZ-AA was best suited to conditions "down home", and was always welcome when captured. With a hammer, welding torch and good intentions, this vehicle could even be rebuilt into a "rail-Zeppelin", as the soldiers jokingly called the rail trucks. This picture shows two vehicles of the 297th I.D. at Shuguyev in the spring of 1942; they brought supplies to the Donetz bridgehead.

More than 9000 of the GAZ-AA were built with ambulance bodies. Here a captured vehicle (with camouflage) has just been cured of motor trouble. The type designation was GAZ-55 (at least for post-1942 models).

A three-axle GAZ-AAA (1.5 tons, 6 x 4, 50 HP) with bus body, used as a staff vehicle. At left is another Ford product, a Ford V8-51, on the "drive" from Krivoi-Rog to Cherson (1st Mtn. Div.).

This GAZ-AAA was used by the 2nd Group of Fighter Squadron 3, as the Roman numeral II under the "WL" shows. The three-axle Russian Ford differed from the two-axle type only in having an additional axle and a somewhat more powerful motor; otherwise it was built exactly the same, and all parts were interchangeable.

The repair truck of Mountain Jäger Regiment 99 in Rostov. A GAZ-AAA with registration WH-705108. Note the division symbol (edelweiss) and camouflage headlights.

Maxim M 1910 quadruple anti-aircraft machine guns with M 31 pillar mount on a GAZ-AAA with dropping tailgate, a welcome prize to Motorcycle Rifle Battalion 19 on the Toropyetz area, September 1941.

Another Russian truck produced in large numbers was the ZIS-5 (3 tons, 4 x 2, 76 HP). Externally it was very much like the GAZ-AA and can be identified chiefly by the asymmetrical middle brace of the front plate. Unfortunately the unit that used this ZIS-5, with a German cross on the side, is not known.

Belgium and France in particular imported many civilian and military trucks to Europe from the USA, or assembled them there. The picture shows a Chevrolet in front of a GMC. By their cabs, both trucks probably came from Belgium.

This 1.5-ton Chevrolet of 1940 may have come from the Netherlands Army, since it had been equipped with vehicles of that type at the beginning of 1940. The picture shows members of the 1st Company of I.R. 398 in Flanders.

It is difficult to tell in which country a Ford truck was built. This one, for example, has the grille of an American 1938 Ford but the standard open cab of the Wehrmacht.

Norway, May 1940: The 2nd and 3rd Mountain Divisions advance together to Bodoe. In the foreground is an American 1.5-ton GMC (built about 1936), small numbers of which were used by the Norwegian Army (with German Notek camouflage headlights). On the street is a Chevrolet, followed by an Opel Blitz with an uncommon cab, an Adler Kübelwagen, a Chevrolet and a Uniform Diesel.

At first glance, it is surprising that this truck of Railway Engineer Regiment 3 could not free itself despite its more than usual off-road equipment. It is a GMC ACK-353 (1.5 tons, 4 x 4, 77 HP), which was delivered to France from the USA in large numbers; its front wheels were prepared for use in desert sand by allowing the attachment of dual wheels. Thus its ground pressure was decreased considerably – but unfortunately, so was the risk to its tires. As a result, the front wheels – despite chains – turned wildly and threw dirt onto even the cover of the handsome truck. (Welikiye Luki area, October 1941).

This GMC (1937-38) was used by the Luftwaffe to transport launcher racks.

This cabover truck, suitable only for flat roads with its extreme overhang, is probably an International COE D 300 (circa 1938) with displaced front axle. The reason for the axle location is really puzzling. The picture was apparently taken in Oslo.

A captured American Mack E Series (1938-39) of Engineer Battalion 216 in Belgium in 1940. At right is a Ford V8-51, apparently also captured, according to its two-piece windshield.

By the spring of 1940 the French Army had bought 1500 White 704 S (3 tons, 4 x 2, 85 HP) trucks from the USA. Large numbers of these outstanding trucks were captured by the Wehrmacht and naturally put to use. Infantry Regiment 51 had at least 15 Whites, which gave loyal service at Staraya Russa. The pictures show WH-893 758 and WH-841 853.

A White 704 S of an unidentified unit. The truck seems to have been sprayed dark yellow.

The French Army had several hundred American trucks of the Studebaker K 25 type. This captured truck was used by Engineer Training Battalion 1 with registration WH-863027, formerly F.P.N. 30189/11.

The Studebaker K 25 was so rugged that a 2 cm Flak gun could be mounted on its rear bed without problems. The "Daumiller Barrage Unit" had at least three of these self-propelled guns in December 1941 and used them successfully in Cyrenaica.

Some 220,000 of the Studebaker US6 (2.5 tons, 6 x 6, 87 HP) were built, mainly for export. Russia alone received over 100,000 trucks of this type, and they were also used as artillery tractors and Stalin Organ carriers. The German troops were naturally happy to capture these fine trucks, even though their fuel consumption of 75 liters per 100 kilometers (off-road) was rather high.

The picture shows a Studebaker in a Hungarian village in 1944, followed by a Peugeot DMA, a Ford and a Uniform Diesel. (BA)

Appendix

Motor Vehicle Numbers

To classify all motor vehicles used by the Wehrmacht, every vehicle was given a vehicle (Kfz.) or special vehicle (Sd.Kfz.) number.

Vehicle numbers were assigned to all unarmored wheeled vehicles, special vehicle numbers to all full- and half-track vehicles and armored wheeled vehicles.

The numbers were assigned by the OKH Weapons Office and gave indication of the intended use of the vehicle, though not of its manufacturer.

During the course of the war, the troops at the front rebuilt countless vehicles (especially captured and stock vehicles), causing a thorough dissipation of this well-intended but overly rigid numbering system. The vehicles introduced as of 1943 (such as sWS, rocket-battery vehicles, etc.) were no longer numbered.

The following list of vehicle numbers reflects their status in 1941. For the sake of completion, personnel vehicles are also included in the list.

Vehicle	Type
1	Light off-road-capable personnel car
1/20	Light off-road-capable amphibian car
2	Radio car
2/40	Small repair service car
3	Light survey troop car
4	Anti-aircraft troop car
5	Medium tank truck
11	Medium off-road-capable personnel car
12	Medium off-road-capable personnel car
13	Machine gun car
14	Radio car
15	Telephone car, cable carrier, radio car, intelligence car
16	Medium survey car
16/1	Alerting vehicle
17	Telephone vehicle, radio vehicle, survey vehicle
17/1	Radio vehicle
18	Combat vehicle
19	Telephone vehicle
21	Heavy off-road-capable personnel car
23	Telephone vehicle

24	Reinforcement vehicle
31	Ambulance
42	Intelligence repair shop truck, collecting vehicle
43	Anti-aircraft fire calculation vehicle
44	Oxygen- and nitrogen-producing vehicle
51	Repair shop vehicle
61	Locksmith vehicle, direction-finding vehicle a, teletype vehicle, telephone service vehicle, radio vehicle, cable measuring vehicle, reinforcement vehicle
61/1	Radio vehicle
62	Print-shop vehicle, light-measuring vehicle, sound-receiving or measuring vehicle, staff evaluation vehicle, survey evaluation vehicle, light weather reporting vehicle
63	Light- or sound-measuring center vehicle, calculation and equipment vehicle, light- or sound-measuring equipment vehicle, measuring equipment vehicle, alerting vehicle
64	Measuring equipment vehicle
68	Radio antenna vehicle, light telephone vehicle
69	Limber
70	Personnel vehicle
72	Medium weather vehicle, print-shop vehicle, telephone or teletype center vehicle, telephone service vehicle, radio vehicle a & b, radio power or listening vehicle, reinforcement vehicle, teletype vehicle
72/1	Teletype vehicle
74	Anti-aircraft fire calculation vehicle
76	Observation vehicle, field cable truck

77	Telephone vehicle
79	Repair-shop vehicle
81	Light anti-aircraft vehicle
83	Light searchlight vehicle I & II
92	Personnel detoxification vehicle
93	Clothing detoxification vehicle
94	Water tank truck
95	Store vehicle
100	3-ton slewing crane on 4.5-ton truck chassis, 5-ton slewing crane on 4.5-ton truck chassis
301	Radio antenna vehicle
302	Radio vehicle
303	Radio surveillance vehicle
305	Medium truck (o) with closed uniform body

The numbers from 300 up were reserved for Luftwaffe vehicles. There were a great many variations of Kfz. 305, their array ranging from "Kfz. 305/1 teletype decoding vehicle" through "Kfz. 305/88 X-ray darkroom chamber vehicle" to "Kfz. 305/137 repair-shop vehicle for aircraft/armament toolmaking." Their bodies differed only in insignificant ways, so that a full listing of them would be unnecessary.

317	Oxygen tank truck
343	Sprayer tank truck
344	Fire hose tender
345	Fire engine
346	Fire hose truck
354	Photography truck
384	Aircraft fuel tank truck
385	Aircraft fuel tank truck
410	Medium anti-aircraft gun truck
415	Anti-aircraft fire survey truck

Motor Vehicle Markings

On February 1, 1942 the following markings were officially instituted in Germany:

WH: Wehrmacht-Heer (Army)WM: Wehrmacht-Marine (Navy)
WL: Wehrmacht-Luftwaffe (Air Force)
RP: Reichspost (Postal Service)
DR: Deutsche Reichsbahn (Railways)
Pol: Polizei (Police)
SS: SS combat and surveillance troops
OT: Organization Todt

Reich Districts and smaller states:

A: Anhalt
IVB: Baden
B: Braunschweig
HB: Bremen
DW: Danzig-Westpreussen
HH: Hamburg
VH: Hessen
K: Kärnten
L: Lippe
M: Mecklenburg
ND: Niederdonau
OD: Oberdonau
Ol: Oldenburg
Saar: Saarland
Sb: Salzburg
SL: Schaumburg-Lippe
St: Steiermark
S: Sudetenland
Th: Thüringen
TV: Tirol & Vorarlberg
P: Wartheland
W: Wien (Vienna)

Prussia:

IA: Berlin Police District
IC: Province of Ostpreussen

IE: Province of Brandenburg
IH: Province of Pommern
IK: Province of Schlesien
IL: District of Sigmaringen
IM: Province of Saxony
IP: Province of Schleswig-Holstein
IS: Province of Hannover
IT: Province of Hessen-Nassau
IX: Province of Westfalen
IY: District of Düsseldorf
IZ: Rhine Province other than
       District of Düsseldorf

Bavaria:

IIA: City of München
IIB: District of Oberbayern
IIC &
IIE: District of Niederbayern &
       Oberpfalz
IID: District of Pfalz
IIH &
IIS: District of Oberfranken &
       Mittelfranken
IIN: Cities of Nürnberg & Fürth
IIU: District of Mainfranken
IIZ: District of Schwaben

Sachsen:

I: Districts of Bautzen, Löbau, Zittau and Kamenz
II: Police of Dresden, Districts of Dresden, Freiberg, Pirna, Meissen, Grossenhain,
      Dippoldiswalde
III: District of Leipzig
IV: District of Chemnitz
V: District of Zwickau

Württemberg:

IIIA: Police of Stuttgart
IIIC: Districts of Backnang, Böblingen, Esslingen
IIID: Districts of Leonberg, Ludwigsburg, Police of Heilbronn
IIIE: Districts of Heilbronn, Vaihingen on the Enz, Waiblingen
IIIH: Districts of Balingen, Calw, Freudenstadt, Horb on the Neckar
IIIK: Districts of Nürtingen, Reutlingen
IIIM: Districts of Rottweil, Tübingen, Tuttlingen
IIIP: Districts of Aalen, Crailsheim
IIIS: Districts of Schwäbisch-Gmünd, Schwäbisch-Hall, Heidenheim, Künzelsau
IIIT: Districts of Bad Mergentheim, Ohringen
IIIX: Districts of Biberach on the Riss, Ehingen (Donau), Göppingen, Ulm
IIIY: Districts of Münsingen, Ravensburg
IIIZ: Districts of Saulgau, Friedrichshafen, Wangen in Allgäu, Police of Ulm

Protectorate:
PA: Böhmen
PB: Mähren-Schlesien
PC: Postal and railroad systems
PD: Prague
PS: Security system
PV: Administrative troops

General Administration: East

As the war extended, there were added:

MB: Military Commander, Belgium and Northern France
MD: Commander of German Troops in Denmark
MF: Military Commander in France
MG: Military Commander in General Administration
MH: Wehrmacht Commander in the Netherlands
MN: Wehrmacht Commander in Norway
MO: Military Commander, Eastern Zone
MR: German Military Mission in Romania
MS: Military Commander, Southeast
MU: Wehrmacht Commander, Ukraine
ZB: Civil Authorities, Belgium and Northern France
ZF: Civil Authorities in France
ZO: Civilian Vehicles in Eastern Operational Zone

Along with official license plates, there were numerous semi-official and personal ones in use. Here are two examples: "RK" for Reichskommissar for the Netherlands" and "WL-N" for the Luftwaffe in Norway.

In hopes of being able to keep captured trucks, the soldiers at first used the field postal number (here with the number 11 added) of their unit. This Studebaker was allowed to remain with the 5th Co., Engineer Training Battalion 1, and saw service at Leningrad with number WH-863027.

The individual Military Zones were assigned groups of numbers for their Wehrmacht vehicles. These applied, though, only in the local zones of the units. For front service, new numbers were always assigned for reasons of secrecy (as of July 3, 1941):

Army:

Zone I Königsberg (Prussia)	WH 10,000-19,999
II Stettin	WH 20,000-29,999
III Berlin	WH 30,000-39,999
IV Dresden	WH 40,000-49,999
V Stuttgart	WH 50,000-59,999
VI Münster (Westfalen)	WH 60,000-69,999
VII München	WH 70,000-79,999
VIII Breslau	WH 80,000-89,999
IX Kassel	WH 90,000-99,999
X Hamburg	WH 100,000-109,999
XI Hannover	WH 110,000-119,999
XII Wiesbaden	WH 120,000-129,999
XIII Nürnberg	WH 130,000-139,999
XIV Magdeburg	WH 140,000-149,999 & WH 240,000-249,999
XV Jena	WH 150,000-159,999 & WH 250,000-259,999
XVI Berlin	WH 160,000-169,999 & WH 260,000-269,999
XVII Linz (Donau)	WH 170,000-179,999
XVIII Salzburg	WH 180,000-189,999

Navy:

Navy High Command, Berlin	WM 1-999
Baltic Naval Stations Command, Kiel	WM 1000- 29,999
North Sea Naval Stations Command, Wilhelmshaven	WM 30,000- 59,999
Commanding Admiral France, Paris	WM 60,000- 79,999
Commanding Admiral Norway, Oslo	WM 80,000- 99,999

Luftwaffe:

Air Zone Command I Königsberg	WL 10,000- 19,999
Air Zone Command Sea Kiel	WL 20,000- 29,999
Air Zone Command III Berlin	WL 300,000-319,999
IV Dresden	WL 400,000-409,999
VI Münster	WL 600,000-609,999
VII München	WL 700,000-709,999
VIII Breslau	WL 800,000-809,999
XI Hannover	WL 110,000-119,999
XIII Nürnberg	WL 130,000-139,999
XVII Wien	WL 170,000-179,999

Tactical Symbols of the Supply Troops

The German vehicles were marked on the front (usually the fender) and rear with symbols that gave information on their ownership within a military unit. These tactical symbols were extremely varied and were often added to or changed by the troops as they saw fit. This chart shows the official situation as of May 1944.

1. Nachschubtruppen

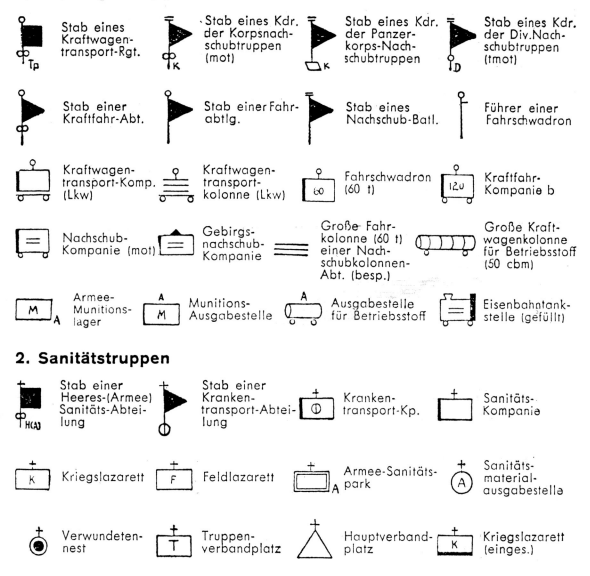

Stab eines Kraftwagen-transport-Rgt.

Stab eines Kdr. der Korpsnach-schubtruppen (mot)

Stab eines Kdr. der Panzer-korps-Nach-schubtruppen

Stab eines Kdr. der Div.Nach-schubtruppen (tmot)

Stab einer Kraftfahr-Abt.

Stab einer Fahr-abtlg.

Stab eines Nachschub-Batl.

Führer einer Fahrschwadron

Kraftwagen-transport-Komp. (Lkw)

Kraftwagen-transport-kolonne (Lkw)

Fahrschwadron (60 t)

Kraftfahr-Kompanie b

Nachschub-Kompanie (mot)

Gebirgs-nachschub-Kompanie

Große Fahr-kolonne (60 t) einer Nach-schubkolonnen-Abt. (besp.)

Große Kraft-wagenkolonne für Betriebsstoff (50 cbm)

Armee-Munitions-lager

Munitions-Ausgabestelle

Ausgabestelle für Betriebsstoff

Eisenbahntank-stelle (gefüllt)

2. Sanitätstruppen

Stab einer Heeres-(Armee) Sanitäts-Abtei-lung

Stab einer Kranken-transport-Abtei-lung

Kranken-transport-Kp.

Sanitäts-Kompanie

Kriegslazarett

Feldlazarett

Armee-Sanitäts-park

Sanitäts-material-ausgabestelle

Verwundeten-nest

Truppen-verbandplatz

Hauptverband-platz

Kriegslazarett (einges.)

3. Veterinärtruppen

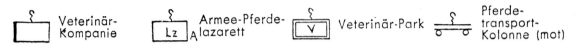

Veterinär-Kompanie

Armee-Pferde-lazarett

Veterinär-Park

Pferde-transport-Kolonne (mot)

4. Kraftfahrparktruppe

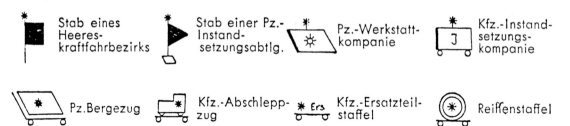

Stab eines Heereskraftfahrbezirks

Stab einer Pz.-Instandsetzungsabtlg.

Pz.-Werkstattkompanie

Kfz.-Instandsetzungskompanie

Pz.Bergezug

Kfz.-Abschleppzug

Kfz.-Ersatzteilstaffel

Reiffenstaffel

Kraftfahrpark

Heimatkraftfahrpark

Gleiskettenlager

Reihen- und Ersatzteillager

5. Feldgendarmerie und Streifendienst

Stab einer Feldgend.Abt. (mot)

Feldgend.-Trupp a (mot)

Stab einer Kdr. einer Streifenabtlg.

Heeresstreife (Offiziersstreife)

6. Trosse

Verpflegungstroß I (mot)

Gepäcktroß

Gefechtstroß einer Art.Abt.

Gefechtstroß einer Pz.Abt.

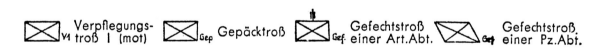

The symbols were most often found as follows: 20 x 10 centimeters, with a letter at the upper left corner (5 cm high) for the troop unit, for example:

T = Technical troops	V = Administrative troops
S = Medical troops	O = Field police
N = Supply troops	Fp = Field post office

To the right of the symbol there was often a more precise identification of the unit, for example: W2 for repair shop company, K1 for column 1, V1 for commissary office, V2 for bakery company, and V3 for butcher platoon, etc.

Troop Symbols

Along with the tactical symbol, most Wehrmacht vehicles also bore more or less carefully painted troop symbols. These symbols usually indicated membership in a certain division, but many regiments and even battalions had their own symbols. The number of different symbols is vast, so that identification often involves considerable difficulty.

Here, as examples, are several hitherto unknown troops symbols of the 20th Mountain Army, as used in 1944.

Commander of Army Supply Troops 463

Medical Troops

Field Artillery Troops

Technical Troops

Motor Vehicle Park Troops

Field Post Office

Administrative Troops

1st Co./Motor Vehicle Transport Regiment 501

Paint Schemes

With the transition from colorful to single-colored field uniforms, eye-catching colors for equipment also began to be avoided, and by 1914, all armies went into the field with their equipment painted gray-green, gray-brown or a similar unobtrusive color. In World War I, attempts were made in particular to make the large equipment (guns, vehicles, etc.) harder for the enemy to see by painting large irregular areas of them in tones of gray, green and brown. This type of painting, known as "mimicry", was then retained by the Reichswehr.

After 1935 the Wehrmacht introduced a new, considerably darker gray-brown paint for equipment. It was chosen because the large equipment was generally set up in forests, villages or under trees, and thus in the shade, and was not supposed to stand out in light colors. The small equipment (canister radios, surveying equipment, etc.) was painted a lighter gray-green.

The ratio of dark gray to dark brown was 2/3 to 1/3. In the autumn of 1939 this paint was in general use, but in 1940 the first change was made.

HM 1940, No. 864:
In order to conserve paint, it was ordered for the duration of the war:
Equipment for which the dark gray/dark brown paint is prescribed is to be painted a solid dark gray.

OKH (Ch.H. Rüst u. BdE), 31/7/1940

HM 1941, No. 281:
Instead of the dark gray/dark brown or solid dark gray paint, the equipment (including all motor vehicles) of the troops in action in Africa should be painted yellow-brown – RAL 8000/gray-green – RAL 7008, with matte (not gloss) paint. This painting is to be done in the same manner as before, instead of dark gray, yellow-brown, instead of dark brown, gray-green is to be used. The colors are not to be contrasted sharply with each other, but must blend into each other gradually. Small surfaces (including wheel spokes and discs) can be painted one color. Yellow-brown is predominant, approximately in the proportion of two thirds yellow-brown to one third gray-green.

OKH (Ch.H. Rüst und BdE), 17/3/1941

HM 1942, No. 315
1. Instead of dark green paint (HM 1940, No. 864), the equipment –including motor vehicles – of the troops in action in Africa should be painted with RAL 8020 brown and RAL 8027 gray paint, both colors with matte (not gloss) paint.

Brown 8020 is dominant, approximately in the proportion of two thirds brown to one third gray. Gray is to be applied in irregular spots, with the two colors blending gradually into each other.

Small surfaces, wheels, etc., can be painted in one color, 8020 or 7027.
The previously used colors, though, 8000 and 7008, are to be used up.

2. Paint that washes off, as stated in HM 1941, No. 1128, is also to be used for painting canvas.

OKH (Ch.H. Rüst u. BdE), 25/3/1942

The order for winter paint in 1941 came much too late. Since the necessary paint colors were largely lacking, the troops often had to use chalk as a camouflage color.

HM 1941, No. 1128
The troops in Norway, on the Finnish front, and in Russia can paint their equipment – vehicles, including motor vehicles, in particular – with white paint for the duration of the snow situation.
The preparation of the paint is entrusted to the troop leaders. Camouflage paint which can be washed off is to be used, according to the altered technical conditions of use as in 6.345. The paint is to be delivered by the troops and the service positions by supply routes. It is to be applied over the existing dark gray paint and washed off when the snow is gone.

OKH (Ch.H. Rüst u. BdE), 18/11/1941

When the hard winter was over, the troops again gave their heavy equipment the prescribed dark gray paint in the spring of 1942. When the second Russian winter began, the troops in the east often had to make do with chalk again. Only the divisions arriving from Germany and the equipment supplied as replacements arrived with white equipment paint.

Only in 1943 were attempts made to regulate the problem of painting equipment anew:

HM 1943, No. 181 (No. 322 is worked in)
1. Equipment paint: Instead of the previous equipment paint, dark gray-dark brown, which has been changed for the duration of the war to solid dark gray, as well as instead of the brown-gray paint for equipment of the troops in Africa and Crete, effective immediately, large equipment is to be painted dark yellow according to example.
For small equipment, which is carried in vehicles (such as intelligence equipment, supply cases, tool boxes, crates and trunks of veterinary equipment, file boxes), the previous paint is to be maintained until further notice. For the painting, the following are to be used:
P paint to TL 6321 for tanks
W paint to TL 6320 for radio and intelligence equipment
Covering paint to TL 6337 for equipment made of magnesium alloys (such as electron wheels on guns)
Otherwise, artificial resin paint to TL 6317 B.
Opposing instructions are no longer applicable.
2. Camouflage paint: The camouflaging of a piece of equipment by applying applicable colors according to prevailing field conditions is a matter for the troops. For this purpose, the troops are to carry camouflage paste (3) in the following colors: olive green in paint boxes of the RLM for camouflage colors (building and ground camouflage), Red-brown, RAL 8017, Dark yellow to pattern, as in #1.
3. The camouflage paste noted in #2 are to be supplied to the troops via supply routes. To calculate the total quantity for every unit, the following average proportions in kilograms may be used:

	Olive Green	Red-Brown	Dark Yellow
Tanks	2.0	2.0	2.0
Personnel cars	0.5	0.5	0.5
Trucks to 2 tons	1.0	1.0	1.0
Trucks over 2 tons	1.5	1.5	1.5

The camouflage paste is issued in packages of 2 and 20 kilograms.

In view of the existing situation as regards raw materials, production and transportation, it must be made the duty of the troops to use paint and camouflage paste cautiously and to limit the consumption to what is urgently necessary.

4. In what form the camouflage paste is to be applied is left to the discretion of the troops. It is generally suitable to divide the surface of a piece of equipment (vehicle) into different colors for purposes of sight.

In general, the application in large spots of color, avoiding all regularity ("cloudy"), has proved effective.

The camouflage paste is to be used in the condition in which it arrives or after the addition of water or gasoline. As well as with a paintbrush, it can also be applied with makeshift tools (brushes, rags), and will dry in a short time. It is also suitable for camouflaging the tarpaulins of trucks.

As far as it is necessary to removed applied camouflage paste, it can be done with gasoline.

5. The winter camouflage (in snow-covered country) consists until further notice of white painting with emulsion paint of TL 6345. All equipment that is issued to the field troops until the end of February 1943 is to be covered with white paint before shipping. The application of white camouflage paint for winter camouflage will be done later.

6. Transitional regulations:

    a) Newly-made equipment which has already been given the previous paint is to be repainted or recolored.

    b) Equipment on hand is only to be repainted with white emulsion paint according to #1 until the end of February 1943.

    c) Among the field troops, the equipment on hand there with dark gray or brown-gray (Africa, Crete) paint is not to be repainted. Necessary camouflaging is to be done with camouflage paste (2 to 4).

    d) Among replacement and occupation troops, equipment is to be painted with new paint as soon as possible, according to #1. The recoloring of truck tarpaulins, though, must be done with camouflage paste.

OKH (Ch.H. Rüst u. BdE), 18/2/1943

This new paint was quickly and universally distributed in the spring of 1943, and provided the German Wehrmacht's typical dark yellow equipment paint of the second half of the year.

The solution of the camouflage problem by the application of camouflage paste over the basic paint was undoubtedly excellent. The troops now had the ability to paint their large equipment in a camouflage color exactly matching the terrain. Unfortunately, though, these instructions were never carried out completely. Quite aside from the shortage of camouflage paste, the necessary quantities of gasoline for applying and washing off the camouflage paste were not available. Fuel was always the chief shortage of the whole German wartime economy. The quantities available were needed for the motor vehicles, and there was none left for camouflage. The application of camouflage paste with water proved to be unworkable, because even the slightest rain washed off the paste that was applied with water.

From 1943 to 1945, the large equipment of the Wehrmacht therefore appeared in dark yellow paint. For the winters of 1943-44 and 1944-45, the troops were supplied at the right times with sufficient white paint.

In the spring of 1945, the dark gray paint began to appear more regularly – obviously for lack of dark yellow paint. In any case, no regulations from this period are available.

The Motor Vehicle Night-Marching Device (Nachtmarschgerät)

The helmet-shaped camouflage headlight was a typical piece of equipment for all Wehrmacht vehicles. Tests with slitted covers in front of the headlights had not given satisfactory results. The camouflage headlight was, of course, supposed to light up the roadway well, but was not supposed to be seen from the air or on the ground. The directed illumination was achieved by using an elliptical rotating reflector, which projected the intensive light from the center of the 35-watt light bulb into the distance and the weaker light from the border area into the vicinity. With the covering hood, no direct light could get out above or to the side. Even from the front, the headlight could be seen only at a distance of 50 meters, and then only when lying flat.

According to the "operating and installing directions" of 1939, the following insight into its construction and use is afforded:

The Vehicle Night-Marching Device has been developed by the Testing Department for Army Motorizing at Wünsdorf in collaboration with the Nova-Technik GmbH of Munich.

The purpose of the device is to provide motor vehicles, singly and in columns, with light at night, without it being possible that they be seen by air or ground observers. In addition, by using the distance taillight (column driving device), it becomes easier to keep columns together.

The Vehicle Night-Marching Device consists of the following parts:

1. The Camouflaged Headlight, which is mounted on the left front fender of the vehicle or between the fender and the motor hood, and illuminates the roadway for a width of some 30-40 meters and a breadth of some 25 meters.

2. The Distance Taillight, which is installed in place of the previous tail- and brake light and is also utilized when driving in columns for estimating intervals.

3. The Step Switch, with which Devices 1 and 2 are switched on or off and the degree of brightness of the camouflage headlight can be adjusted.

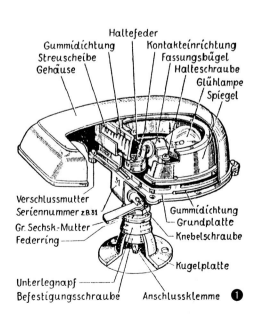

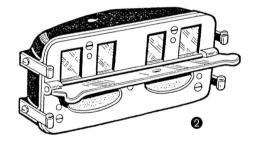

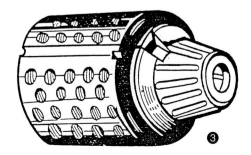

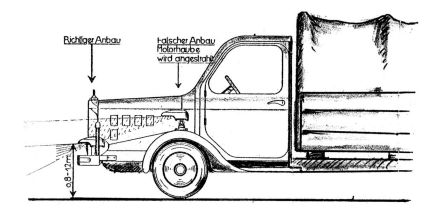

The degree of brightness of the camouflage headlight can be adjusted by several switch settings:

Setting O = Camouflage headlight and distance taillight turned off.

Setting H = Headlight off, only taillight on: used for column driving when driving must be done completely without headlights to avoid being seen by the enemy, or when only the leading vehicle of the unit is to drive with headlight. Observation from the air is not possible, from the ground only to a distance of 300 meters.

Setting V1 = Headlight at its lowest strength, taillight on: used on very dark nights in the vicinity of the enemy, for example, used as a matter of course when driving to battery positions, taking up readiness positions, etc. Air and ground observation beyond 500 meters impossible. On somewhat brighter nights, the V2 setting can be used without danger in place of V1, though not in the immediate vicinity of the enemy.

Setting V2 = Headlight medium bright, taillight on: used near and behind the front, for example, when advancing to the front, transferring motorized units. Air and ground observation beyond 800 meters impossible.

Setting V3 = Headlight at full strength, taillight on: used when driving on blackout drills in peacetime or in peacetime drills on public roads. Air and ground observation over approximately 1500 meters impossible.

Important! Since the camouflage headlight does not indicate the width of the vehicle, the parking lights of the main headlights or the side position lights must be on. Driving is to be done with parking lights, never with high or low beams!

The Distance Taillight consists of a combination of the rear light which illuminates the license plate, the brake light and the distance light. For the sake of blacking out the vehicle, the vertical flap on the tail- and brake lights is folded down and the lever for the window of the license-plate light is pushed closed.

The effect of this device for estimation of the distance to the vehicle in front depends on the perceptive ability of the human eye, which recognizes several points of light close together as actually separated only within certain distances. The process is as follows: The distance taillight produces a strongly subdued light which is recognizable as a point of light to the following driver up to 300 meters away. When approaching more closely (catching up), the driver recognizes two fields of light at about 35 meters, and at a distance of 25 meters, all four fields of light finally appear as clearly separated from each other. The driver in the column can thus recognize the distance from the preceding vehicle and keep the usual column distance of 25 to 35 meters.

Motor Vehicles in Winter

The extremely cold winter of 1941-42, with temperatures of -43 degrees and more Celsius, caused simply insoluble problems for the motorized troops in particular.

Flying snow and frozen slush caused tracks and wheels to literally freeze fast to the ground; cables, brakes and moving parts refused to work. Oil and grease solidified and lost their lubricating ability. Diesel fuel thickened and plugged the lines. Even gasoline lost its capability to form an ignitable mixture. The batteries lost their electricity and even froze when at a low charge. Engine blocks and radiators were cracked by frozen cooling water, because no anti-freeze was available and the water could not be drained off at the right time. With the few vehicles that could be started, the drivers had a very hard fight to drive through snowdrifts and over sheet ice, generally doing so in completely unheated, drafty cabs.

The makeshift measures ordered by the OKH were necessarily too late for the first Russian winter.

The 130 pages of instructions in D 635/5, "Motor Vehicles in Winter", were a subsequent attempt to tackle the problems. How that was to be done will be shown by citing points from the edition of 7/7/1943:

1. Special fuel for the eastern front, winterized to take temperatures to -40 degrees C: gasoline (colored purple), Diesel fuel (tank trucks and containers marked with a big white "W"), special, easily ignited starting fuel (kerosene) for gasoline motors.

2. "Motor oil of the Wehrmacht (winter)", which could be mixed with 15% fuel at temperatures under -20 degrees C, and with 25% fuel (gasoline or Diesel) at temperatures below -3) degrees C.

3. "Fuel oil of the Wehrmacht 8 E", colored green, pumpable to -40 degrees C, will be delivered as of autumn 1943. Previously the fuel oil had to be thinned with gasoline.

4. "Lubricating grease of the Wehrmacht" becomes stiff at low temperatures as before, and is to be mixed with motor oil at a ratio of 1:1.

5. Special parts to be installed, classified for all types of vehicles in use as so-called large (with heater for cold water) or small (without heater for cold water) winter kits, with:

– Heater for batteries (the battery came in a sheet-metal case that was heated with an alcohol lamp)
– Easily removable battery clamps (for quick battery removal)
– Starting fuel container with two-way spigot (the special fuel –0.5-1.0 liter – allowed easier starting but had to be turned off during driving to avoid danger of fire
– Cold-water heater (a small heat exchanger was connected to the cooling system by tubing. The warming of the heat exchanger was done by a spirit lamp)
– Heat lamp (running on gasoline or kerosene, the most important device for winter operation. It was used to heat cold water, ventilator covers, heating funnels, batteries, starters, gears and the like and was sometimes very overused)
– Cab heating (by additional heat exchangers and ventilators or by "heating ovens for vehicle bodies" for solid fuel)

6. For the starting of motor vehicles when all inherent means of starting failed, the presence of an adaptable "uniform turning crank" was necessary. To this there could then be attached:

– The crankshaft gasoline starter (KBA), consisting of a portable combustion motor with two-speed gear and sliding clutch
– The motorcycle crankshaft starter (KKA), consisting of one gear with two friction rollers, which were driven by the hind wheel of a motorcycle
– The SS starting device, Rumpler pattern, was operated only by muscle power via two hand cranks intended for a two- to eight-man crew.

In crude practice, an open fire (usually Diesel fuel in a metal pan) was placed under the motor and gearbox and the vehicle was thus warmed (in the Russian manner). The first vehicle that was started then had the job of starting other vehicles by towing them. This method was damaging, to be sure, but effective, and the instructions cited above were certainly not inspired by it.

Finally, it must be noted that our modern, present-day motor vehicles would have unsuspected difficulties at temperatures below -43 degrees Celsius!

Heating the battery in the warming box by means of a wick lamp; the front wall has been removed.

In the Ford V 3000 S, the heat exchanger (5) of the cooling-water heater was located behind the right front fender and was warmed by the heat lamp.

Motor Vehicles in Dust, Sand and Heat

When the German Afrika-Korps landed in North Africa in February 1941, considerable technical problems for motor vehicles confronted the troops.

The high air temperatures and the hot rays of the sun had very disadvantageous effects on the vehicles:

The German motor oil became so thin that the engines seized; the cooling water, difficult to obtain, turned to steam and evaporated in no time – as did the battery fluid. Gasoline (though not Diesel) tended to form air bubbles in the fuel lines and evaporated in considerable quantities. At ground temperatures of 65 to 80 degrees Celsius, the rubber tread loosened from the fabric of the tires. Vehicle parts made of wood, rubber or plastic (especially on account of the great differences between day and night temperatures) became cracked, brittle and unusable.

The vehicles' worst enemies, though, were the dust and sand of sharp-angled quartz; moving parts in motors, gearboxes, generators, etc. were abraded and ruined, fuel lines and cooling ducts were plugged, the electric systems shorted out.

The chief measures listed in D 635/50 (as of 10/1/1942) were the following procedures, which could basically be carried out in Germany:

Linen coverings over the oil-bath air filter or installation of a felt-bellows air filter, application of additional thickeners or protective coatings to oil-filler openings, oil dipsticks, cylinder heads, gearboxes, steering and brake parts and all cables, sealing all observation and servicing openings. Alkor tablets were to be added to the cooling water to prevent scale deposits and salty water.

According to these instructions, "special equipment for the troops" was developed for the following vehicles:
1. Light Pkw K1 Type 82 (VW Kübel)
2. Light Pkw Type 40 (light uniform car)
3. Medium Pkw Type 40 (medium uniform car)
4. Steyr 1.5-ton truck
5. Opel Type 6700 A

According to manufacturers' data, this special equipment also existed for at least the heavy uniform car and the Ford V 3000 S. Stock vehicles had to be provisionally modified by the troops for use in the tropics.

Wood-Gas Power

In Germany's efforts to be independent of imported petroleum, the Reich government gave contracts to the industry at an early date to develop vehicle power systems involving the use of domestic fuels. The fuels available were wood, charcoal, lignite, anthracite and the like. The outbreak of war hastened the development and use of these so-called gas generators to a great degree. The most widely used fuel was wood, which was to be distributed to more than 3000 (planned) wood filling stations by the "Society for Fuel Wood Acquisition and Waste Wood Evaluation AG." On May 30, 1942, the "Central Office for Generators" was founded: there was now liquid fuel only for front-line vehicles, party, police and other such vehicles, while wood-gas generators were planned for all vehicles back home.

By the end of the war, some 200,000 wood-gas generators were produced and used chiefly by the replacement army (there were even driving-school tanks with wood-gas drive), the RAD, the OT, the NSKK and licensed private firms.

The principle of the wood-gas generator is:

Into an upright boiler are placed air-dried, fist-size blocks of wood and heated in the absence of air. The resulting, highly poisonous CO gas is sucked by the motor via filter, cooler and carburetor and ignited by spark plugs. Basically, every gasoline or Diesel engine could be modified to run on wood-gas by installing the right parts.

The preparation, cleaning and particularly starting with the blower were a very laborious and dirty job. The leading manufacturer in Germany was the firm of Imbert in Cologne.

The fuel consumption of a 5-ton truck for 100 kilometers was 100 kilograms of beechwood or 50 kilograms of anthracite.

The performance deficit of the motors was stated as approximately 20%.

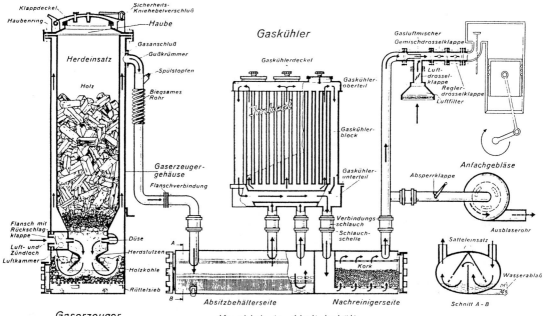

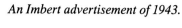

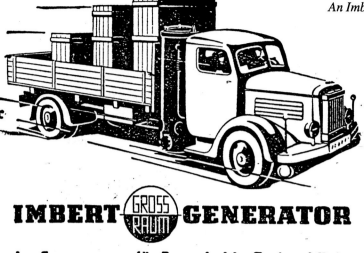

IMBERT GROSS RAUM GENERATOR

der Gaserzeuger für Braunkohle, Torf und Holz, einsatzfähig im europäischen Großraum.

Tests of the suitability of wood-gas vehicles by the Reichswehr and then by the Wehrmacht gave unsatisfactory results. The picture shows a Hansa-Lloyd "Merkur" with a Deutz wood-gas system, Type KU 207. Note the chamber gas filter, the bumper used as a duct, and the fine design of the gas cooler.

The Motor Vehicle Service Medal

In recognition of the wartime service of particularly capable drivers, the OKW/FHQ instituted motor vehicle service medals in bronze, silver and gold versions on October 23, 1942. The guidelines for awarding are stated in abridged form below. It certainly was not simple to win this small, unobtrusive medal, which was worn on the lower left sleeve!

Required was service under particularly difficult conditions
as a motorcycle messenger: on 90 days in action,
as a combat vehicle driver: on 120 days in action,
as a driver in Trains I & II, columns and staffs: on 150 days in action,
as a driver of supply-troop vehicles: on 165 days in action,
as a driver for other Wehrmacht services and units: on 185 days in action.

As days in action, documentation of difficult conditions for delivery and maintenance included:

Travel under enemy fire,
Particularly great daily achievement in terms of distance and time or particularly difficult road conditions, or
Trips under unusually rough weather conditions.

Despite these difficult conditions, the drivers had to have stood out through superior and careful driving and conscientious vehicle maintenance and service.

In the event of an accident that was the driver's fault, the previously evaluated days in action became invalid. Days in action could then be counted after six months of trouble-free driving.

The Motor Vehicle Service Medal could be withdrawn because of:

– proved careless maintenance, servicing and driving of the vehicle, which led to premature damage to the vehicle,
– the driver's being at fault in an accident because of careless and thoughtless handling of a motor vehicle,
– punishment for exceeding the prescribed top speed.

The Motor Vehicle Service Medal was awarded to:

– drivers of the Wehrmacht,
– drivers (not Wehrmacht members) subordinated to the Wehrmacht,
– drivers (not Wehrmacht members) used in areas occupied by the Wehrmacht,

The medal could also be awarded to:

– foreign volunteers, under oath to the Führer, fighting in the German Wehrmacht,
– foreigners from the eastern regions liberated from the Bolsheviks (including freed prisoners of war), as long as they fought under the command of the German Wehrmacht.

Awarding the medal to members of the armed forces of allied or friendly countries was not allowed.

A major injustice was done in the treatment of ambulance drivers! At first they could not be awarded the medal at all, and only rather late, on May 24, 1943, were they made equal to supply-train drivers and could receive the medal after 150 days in action.

Hard-nosed, rugged and talented at scrounging: this motto surely applied not only to this Krupp truck crew but to the drivers of all nations.